Small Business Marketing 101

- Better Sales, Bigger Profits, Enjoying Freedom

by Robert Kintigh

Truth Mastery
P.O. Box 582
Cool, CA 95614

Table of Contents

1. Acknowledgements

I am very grateful for everything that I have experienced in my life as it has afforded me the opportunity to be able to express myself as an author and as a speaker and trainer. I have many people to thank along the way but most importantly I thank God for the gifts I have been given and the opportunity to use them.

 Life has so much to offer and I am ready, willing and able to share what I know and have learned. I am also very thankful for you my readers who continue to support me. I cannot thank you enough and I hope to repay you with some great information, ideas and value that help you in your pursuit of growing a business.

I dedicate to all of the customers, clients and sales people I have had the pleasure to work with over the years. I have learned so much both good and bad and without the time we spent together, the work I had to put in to learn and the dedication of everyone working together has come together to create books like this in order to help other.

I have enjoyed all of the sales experiences that I have had both on the small level, corporate sales, network marketing and running my own businesses. Sales have been a huge part of my life and without the skills I learned I would have never been able to achieve the great life that I live today. Thank you to each and every one of you who have helped me grow along the way as I am forever in your debt and this book is just one way of giving back.

I also want to acknowledge all of the mentors I have never met in my life as I have spent my life time learning from you on CD, books and seminars. If there is one thing I have learned along the way is that to be successful I must always have a thirst for learning, always be open to changing my ways when they are not the best and do everything with passion.

I want to thank teachers who I have had along the way as well from High School to College I have taken much of what I have learned and put it to good use. I thank you for the dedication and the relentless time you served my classmates and me.

As always, I appreciate the support and love that my family provides. My success is as much tied to you as my work experience is. I am grateful that I have a love for writing and helping people as both of these actions gives me great pleasure in my life.

If we have crossed paths along the way I want you to know that no matter the outcome of our relationship I have paid attention to the time we have spent together and deliver it back in the way of this book. I thank you for everything and I hope that you understand the admiration I have for the lessons I learned. Take this information and use it, pass it along and my hope is you cherish the outcome. Thank you and I wish you only the best.

2. Introduction

If you are like most small businesses, your dreams came to life one day when you realized you were tired of working for someone else and decided you were going to start your own business. You had no idea how you were going to do it, but you were determined to make it happen. You were not concerned with the small details as you had great ideas as to how the office would look or the showroom floor. You focused on products or services and what they would do for people. You were ecstatic to finally be an entrepreneur and the excitement in your heart was electric. Then the reality hit you square in the face that there was more to be done than just setting up shop or your home office.

If small businesses fail within 3-5 years and people fail in network marketing in 30-90 days, what do you think could be some contributing factors to this happening? I know things like being underfunded and failing to plan fall at the top of the list. You will have to work on the funding part but the planning part is my specialty at least for this book.

When we fail to plan our business, we end up with what we end up with and most of the time it is not very special. A businesses' soul identity is what is built into their brand. A brand is carefully planned for and executed and no part of the details should be skipped over. In this book we will take you through what you are going to need to understand to brand your business. In the meantime, I hope that you are excited to be going on this journey with me so that you can discover the best ways to build your brand on line and take your business to a whole new level.

There are many who have come before you and many that will come after you and many of these people will never take the time to do what I am talking about. Some will have success by luck and some will fail miserably. Those who will take the time to plan and design their brand will have the highest chance possible if building something very special.

How do you brand yourself on line? I will do everything in my power to give you all the information you will need in order to create your own brand on line. It will be up to you to make it happen and follow what I have for you. Start out simple and then move towards something more sophisticated if you so desire but keep track of your brand on line. Do not worry about the negative impact any more than the positive as both will have to be managed and addressed.

Many people today worry about social media because of the complexity of the platforms and the fear of negative feedback. My hope is that I will get you to see that no matter what you believe, the Internet is your playground and you will have fun if you let yourself be free with the creative process. Social media, websites, blogs, video channels and more are here to allow you complete freedom to create a look that you can be proud of. The only limitations are the ones that you will put in front of you.

What you should be seeking is everything from branding, to websites, to employee training and more. This book has what you need and your excitement will come back. Now, let's get ready to learn how to brand you or your company on line!

3. Learn to Brand Yourself Online

In today's World where there is so much noise both on and offline, it is becoming more and more important to separate our company and image from the rest of the crowd and to get noticed for being unique. In this book called "How to Brand Yourself Online," we will explore what our brand should look like, how we are going to manage our brand and what tools we should use to build and maintain our image. I am writing this book because I am seeing more and more companies diluting any hope of a brand that is recognizable. We are following others like sheep and not going on our own pathway. We will teach you how to brand yourself online and create a winning look.

Before the internet, creating a strong brand meant having a lot of money as you really had only 3 ways to get your brand out there in the world; one was media, two was print and the third was word of mouth. The first two took lots of money and the third meant spending long hard time working at it. For a small business this would prove to be challenging and most had to resort to the third option as most small businesses never had the budget large enough to capture television or print. Since the internet and mobile marketing has come around, a small business now has the capabilities to do more than ever before.

Branding is the constant re-enforcement of how you want people to see your company. Branding comes in many shapes, sizes, colors and looks. Branding tells a story about your business. It is something that needs to be consistent yet so few small businesses seem to get right. It is a long term strategy of putting your business out into the general public so that they will be able to identify you by colors, style, pictures, words and products or services. It is a well thought out play that makes complete sense as to who you are and want to be seen as. In short, your brand is both your visual and written presentation and communication that speaks to your prospects and customers about who and what you are about.

We will talk about some of the obvious big companies and their brands and maybe some of the ones that are not so big and obvious. We will talk about how most have tried a color and it has never worked yet this incredible company has made it work for them and their simple slogan around it. We will point out some of the big mistakes small companies make and how you can avoid them.

Your brand should be the beginning point to launching your company at least in concept and in every face of it that you deploy into the world. Do not have the idea that you will work on it later or fix it later when it comes to creating and designing your brand. Start off your company right from the beginning or stop what you are doing and fix it now and not later. Every message that you put out should tell a story and if you do not have one well-crafted then your prospects and customers will be confused or turned off.

No matter if you are a small business, an author, attorney, band, musician, or a number of other small businesses, what you look like to your prospects or customers will determine how they respond to your offerings. There are different ways to build your brand depending on what it is that you represent but essentially the basics and principles all come down to a similar path taken to establish the brand. Get ready to learn from someone with 22 years of experience in business that has built several brands both big and small for a small business. I give up my secrets, tips, ideas, ways to operate on a budget when you need to, posting on Facebook and social media and so much more. How to Brand Yourself Online is a book that will try and answer for you as many questions that you may have about branding and why some things are very important and why some are not so important.

Pull out a pen and some paper and take notes as you begin to read this book. No matter if you are new to business or are a veteran, I promise that I have much to teach you and provide for you as we go along. In order to be good at branding, you need to pay attention to the companies who have done it right as well as those who have failed and I have spent years paying attention. Once you finish this book, get ready to go to work and create the best brand possible for your company.

Before we dive in, let me ask you one quick question; "Can you describe what your business does in one sentence?" If the answer is yes, then I applaud you and celebrate a great starting point. If the answer is no then you have some work to do. People are going to ask you all the time what your company does and they will not hang on for a 30 minute diatribe on what you think your company is about. They will definitely get lost in the "ums and the uhs" so think about a one liner that is crisp and to the point! For instance, my marketing company helps brand small businesses so that their prospects and customers know what they do!

What we are ultimately doing is trying to build what is called a platform. A platform is what it sounds like, something that you use to connect to the world with. All of the offerings of your company make up your platform and the brand is the face of it all. A platform gives you a podium of sorts to speak to the world and be seen. When we talk about everything in this book to do with branding your company online, we are really talking about all of the pieces that make up your brand and extend your platform.

Platforms are commonly used all the time by coaches, authors and speakers. They are always trying to build their platform so that they can gain more exposure. Ultimately, they are trying to do the same thing that you need to do. Build a good company face and look and then reach out as far as they can with their voice.

Not everyone needs to be an internet marketing expert to build their brand online. When you have the basic understanding of what you need and how to do it, then you will be well on your way. At some point you may need to enlist the help of an expert to fine tune your brand, but upfront if money is tight, do what you can and proceed with some caution. Do not cause your brand any harm.

Branding online will take you some time so make sure you have some patience. All too often we get clients who think everything can be done online in 30 days or less. They believe there are magic buttons we push and all is easy and done. By the second month they think they should be all set and that no more money will need to be spent. Nothing is further from the truth, as once you start you will never stop if you are smart. Professionals constantly work on their brand. Keep refining your brand and make sure you leave nothing unturned.

3.1. What is in a Brand?

When we talk about branding a business, there are certainly many elements that go into creating the complete picture. As I have already asked about your one liner, there are many things you will want to create and design around the main theme of what you do or are about. What is in a brand is everything from images, graphics, your elevator pitch, your tag line, your handouts, website, social media, and mobile app and so on. How far you go or what all is involved in your branding effort is up to you. Let's take a look at where to start if you are a new business or where to start if you are an existing business.

If you are like most small businesses then resources are a concern. You cannot attack everything you need up front and that is okay as long as you are prepared up front and have a long term game plan. Plan it out in advance and then execute as the resources become available. I know you have so much to do and that the time could be used for painting the new walls or picking up supplies or a number of other things but I assure you that this kind of thinking will only hurt you later. You need the most well rounded offering planned out in advance and then you can make it happen as resources become available.

There are many ways that you can begin to design your brand. You might start with your company colors, a logo, a tag line or your products or services. You will ultimately decide, but we will walk you through designing based upon some generic set of ideas and choices so that you will have an idea how to get to where you need to.

We are going to first talk about company colors. Where a lot of small businesses make a mistake with company colors is they choose colors they like, have seen another company use or just plain guess on the colors they want to use. There are many things we could talk about when it comes to colors for your company, but let's start with understanding how colors work to express our company. Blues are always a favorite for most companies because it is pleasant to the eye and lends itself to a professional look.

Too many colors lend itself generally to a childish look which may not be what you are shooting for. Colors create moods in people and also can either elevate the look of your business or lower it drastically. I like starting with the colors of the company first because they will come into play with many of your company's offerings such as the logo, the website, business cards and so much more. There is no right or wrong place to start but in my mind colors is where I suggest everyone to start with.

Once you have done your research and decided on your company colors, then onto designing the logo. Here is an area that is really interesting to me as so many small businesses try to do too much and say too much for whatever reason. I believe it is because they lack an understanding of an overall branding package or plan for their company and they think every piece needs to be a novel instead of a short story that is part of a series. A logo can just be an image with your company colors. Do you remember the Golden Arches? Your logo could be just a word or two with 2 colors. Need I remind you of the company Coca Cola? Most small businesses try to cram too many words, some over- thought image, and too many colors to create their logo. They never consider how it will look on a business card or T-shirts or letterhead. Be smart and make an impact with something that is clean and crisp. Do not create a logo that is too busy as it will only be confusing.

From here it is up to you what to do next. Perhaps a website or Facebook Fan page would be in your budget or timeline. You will want to keep everything you do consistent. You might even consider writing policy and procedure on how all aspects of your branding is executed should it need to be replicated in the future. When this is done you will spell out everything like pantone colors, printing companies that you can use paper or signs, sizes, etc. Nothing will be trivial when you do this. We will talk more about this in the next section and spell out what the big companies do.

How do some companies get people to fall in love with their brand? If I could tell you this then every company in the world would have it made. What I can do is point some things out like I have in this book so far that make it easier to fall in love with your brand. There is definitely no formula or exact recipe to make this happen. For Microsoft and Bill Gates, he made desktop computers easier to use and a whole lot more fun to operate. Apple and Jobs made their brand special and unique.

McDonald's created Ronald and fun meals in a box for kids. Some companies donate to charities and help feed the homeless. Some companies help support school and give away college scholarships.
You will have to follow your heart and then pay attention and ask questions of your customers to figure out the puzzle. One thing I have learned over the years is that if you will ask your customers and are willing to listen, then they will let you know both good and bad. People love to be heard and love it when people actually care. When people love your brand they will become fanatical and will contribute to your bottom line.

Packaging is very important when you are trying to brand, even online. You must take care with every aspect and not leave any detail out. If you have products and you want to show them off online, the packaging and look need to be sharp in order for prospects to want to buy. Most consumers' love great packaging and it will showoff itself online.

When your company package arrives at their home or office, you want the expectations to match what they saw. Photoshop will not work if the packaging is different upon arrival. We always suggest using a professional with any type of graphics which includes packaging or web images. You may have great products but with poor graphics you will sell very little.

3.2. What Do the Big Companies Do?

As we last discussed, big companies will create policy and procedure in regards to how their branding is to be handled and executed. They will spell out everything as they want to make sure that they keep everything they do consistent, of high quality and they leave nothing open to be guessed about. Will this be the difference between you and the big corporation? Will you be too busy to spell everything out? Will you not take the time to commit it to writing and standards? Big business understands how important this kind of planning and commitment is and if you want to compete and build a billion dollar brand then maybe you will take note.

Big companies also have committees who give input on what is being deployed. If you are too small then find a group of people whom you know and respect who do not mind helping out. Weigh out their input but these should be people with the appropriate backgrounds. It looks pretty may not exactly be what you are in need of. Someone who will agree with you and not be brutally honest is not helpful. Recruit those who will be the most helpful, honest and are properly educated in business or marketing.

Big companies never use the words "Good enough." They work on things until they are exactly the way that they want them. They use things like story boards and idea sessions to march towards what they want in a look. You may have to adjust based upon your resources but one way or another use vision and creativity to create your brand. There are already plenty of ordinary and horrible and fragmented brands out in the world today. You can join the ranks of the elite who actually prepare and care for their brands. What Can Brown Do for You is a slogan and color made famous by UPS and is one of the toughest colors ever to use in business, but as you have seen UPS has no issue making it work. Brown trucks, clothes, company colors and more are all done in the name of brown! Big companies will often take risk on something and will see it through to the end. This can be a great thing most of the time but can also blow up in their faces. There are a ton of color experts out there that will tell you that brown is not a suggested color to brand your company with and they are probably right but as I see my UPS person pull up to my office, I have no doubt who it is from the second I see that brown truck.

How does United Parcel Service or UPS make it work? Branding of course! They have trained me and you and everyone else to know what it stands for including my children. In fact, my children almost think of UPS as Christmas all year round when that truck pulls up, they equate that brown truck to bringing presents and goodies. Do you think you could make brown work for you? Do you think you can train your customers to know what you are about? If the big companies can do it then so can you in whatever size your world is!

Lastly, big companies keep everything consistent and do not change their brand look every six months. Once they have developed a look or offering, they understand that they need to get it out there in front of people over and over again so that it can be recognized from miles away. My oldest son could spot the Golden Arches I swear five miles out. He was trained by two years old what that M stood for. That is brilliant branding and no matter what you think about the nutrition of the food, the look is a lean, mean branding machine! This symbol is already taken but who knows what you can come up with? The possibilities are endless and I am sure by now you are starting to come up with all kinds of ideas. Let's move on to how you are going to utilize social media for branding purposes.

3.3. Branding Using Social Media

Social media has evolved in a very short time period. It has gone from silly kids' stuff to a powerful business tool like no other. From a branding stand point of view, it does something very well if utilized properly. You can extend your brand in a way that I call drip marketing. You can constantly put out little messages that make up a bigger message in a consistent way. Mistakes that I see on social media all the time is that too many small businesses get in a hurry and blast people with a message that seems to have no direction. Branding on Social media has to be carefully crafted, managed and deployed with a beginning and end in mind. Let me explain what I mean.

Social media, especially sites like Facebook, Twitter, LinkedIn, Pinterest, and YouTube have a captivated audience. There are people showing up here on a daily basis and they are there for your company to show off your brand. People on social media love to share and will do so if you will give them something interesting, heartfelt or something that adds value. A poor graphic and a boring tagline will not turn heads. Drip your message to people so they know what you are all about. Have a theme so that everything you put out marches people to a stronger understanding about your company image.

It is important to keep a close eye on your social media campaigns and make sure your brand is being deployed as you wish. Things can get out of control very quickly on social media sites and often times no one is paying attention. People will share both what they like and things they do not like so it would be very wise to understand this idea and what it will take to keep your company in good light. Again, writing down policy for social media is very important both for the company and employees as well because if they post that they work at your company or organization (which is a good thing if done right) you want to make sure that they do not post things that will diminish the company or them.

So how do you go to work on your brand on social media? Just like the Great Wall of China, you will build it one stone at a time. Let people see your logo and your tag line. Create videos that intro your company and post graphics that tell a simple picture. Social media has gone very visual so images and videos are very powerful tools. Go to work creating relationships and make sure that your profile or page shows off your brand. Make everything top notch and make sure not to post anything unprofessional. Share other peoples stuff and tell why you like it. Align yourself with other companies who are quality and that have a good following and support the relationship with like-minded things!

Social media can be a very good commercial to consistently get your brand out into the public's eye as long as you have a plan. Take note: if you are a new brand, you will need to start from the beginning. As an established business you have the ability to extend your brand even more.

Social media is a sharing tool so keep that in mind and always try to put out things that are share worthy. You can do good deeds and have your brand attached. Write a story, news episodes, facts, interesting articles, giving and more. Tell a story on social media of what you are about and you will find that many will share your story. Have patience and reap the rewards of your hard work.

3.4. Branding on the Mobile App

We can't talk about branding these days without mentioning the mobile app industry. A company in Walnut Creek California called GenEpoch has coined the phrase that the mobile app is the new internet. If this is the case, then we need to include branding on mobile devices just as important as branding on line. With this new technology, we are seeing a game changer and just like the race for the internet to stake a claim on line with a website, this race will be even bigger.

A mobile app is a bit different than a website. In order to properly brand yourself on mobile apps we need to understand how they work and what they will do for you. Mobile apps are being downloaded by the millions. There have been 25 Billion apps downloaded to date and by the year 2015 experts predict that there will be 183 billion. This is happening because people are captivated by their mobile apps. Most people have their mobile device within reach 24 hours a day.

The fueling of smartphone sales and the tiny app icons that people are so mesmerized over on those phones are bringing about one of the biggest revolutions in history. Since 2007, mobile apps have been reserved for the companies and entertainers who can afford them as price tags have reached upwards of one hundred thousand dollars. This has held back small businesses from being able to take place in this incredible marketing tool. This has now all changed.

Today, the small business owner has new options for getting in front of the mobile crowd. Platforms are coming about and more affordable options like the ones being offered by GenEpoch. Today a small business can get an app as low as $200.00 for a self-design option and up to fifteen hundred dollars. These prices are just samplings but I am sure that you are getting the picture. With the explosion of all of this and now the price becoming very affordable, you can now start on a new, powerful road branding your company on mobile devices.

A mobile app is supposed to be a marketing tool that will do a number of things, but first and foremost it should create a call to action as well as extend your brand. We will talk about the brand and look of the app and what I am seeing in the industry. Since the industry is new for small business, especially with the advent of self-design platforms, I am seeing some very bad mobile apps. The graphics that are being produced are disorganized and not very effective. Like all marketing pieces that represent your company, care needs to be taken to ensure that the brand is extended and not harmed.

Apple has set standards to try and make sure that the mobile apps that are submitted to Apple are done well. What this means for you is that you take your time and produce or have produced a high quality app that is dynamic and well-constructed. If you want to know more about apps, then I suggest you get one of my other books on Amazon called The Mobile App Revolution for Small Business (you can search Amazon for the title or by my name Robert Kintigh).

This book will spell out more about mobile apps, but what I want to make as clear as possible is that when you get your mobile app designed, it is something that is memorable and has a greater purpose. The graphics need to be professional and the design match the look of your company. Logo needs to be high resolution and consistent. Don't rush the look of it as right now you will be a pioneer by having your own mobile app for your company. Give them the very best look possible and do not degrade your brand.

3.5. Does Your Graphics Really Matter?

Graphics are often the first thing people recognize about a company. Just as I had talked about the Golden Arches earlier, people recognize symbols and images of some of the biggest companies in the world. Don't you believe your company can be the same? If the answer is yes then you must get creative and make it happen. If you do not believe that you cannot do the same thing then ask yourself why not? Why re-invent the world when all of the big companies have already shown you the way. They have spent millions to get the right formula and all you have to do is come up with your own version.

I know that you are a small business and money is always an issue. I understand that you are always looking for ways to do things on your own and save some money. I do not wish to sound insensitive by any means but do not try to pinch a penny by doing your own graphics if you do not have the skill to do so. Pinch pennies where it might make more sense, but the branding of your business is not to be sacrificed.

Yes, graphics matter and the sooner that you own up to this idea, the sooner you will make sure that only top notch images, graphics and videos are put out by your company. You will agree to have only the best look and good enough only hurts your brand. When you are ready to put it out there online, become a tough critic and let others put an eye on what you are launching. When it is right, then let it launch!

There are plenty of ways to get great graphics done for your company. There is the lower end side of Fiverr where you can get graphics for as low as five dollars. There are websites where people will compete for your work which tends to help you save a ton of money. There are also plenty of up and coming graphic artist companies out there that want to get noticed and will work below rate. If you have the resources then there are some top notch firms that will give you a very professional and dynamic look.

A good graphic artist can cost you upwards of $250.00 an hour but the cost is worth it as this is the look of your company and the professionalism is generally on a whole new level. No matter what you pay for your graphics make sure they are what you want for your brand; they are sharp, crisp and that the graphic company sends them to you in different sizes and file formats.

Before we wrap up this subject, I want to ask you a question, "what is more powerful on a first impression on line?" Words are great, but the biggest first impression is your graphics. Everything is important with your offering, but an image is worth a thousand words. What does your image say to the on line world? Show off your best side and do not be afraid to take a chance.

Robert D. Kintigh

4. The Best Way to Brand Your Company Online

Ever wonder what would be the best way to brand your company online? I always say that the best way to brand yourself online is to do your research. What you are looking for is a niche or a theme or a look that is not overly saturated. There are millions of samples out there for you to examine and see what you like. Look at a ton of logos and graphics. Check out tag lines and the font that they use. Read through their websites and see what you like and what you dislike. Check out small business mobile apps and how they are laid out.

Take notes of the stuff you really like and discover why you like it. Take notes of the stuff you really hate and discover why you hate it. Sometimes you just need some ideas provided to you so you can ultimately create your own masterpiece. You need to create something that people identify with and enjoy dealing with. You need to find that winning combination that says so much about your company.

When I was growing my service/construction business, I searched high and low for messages that appealed to me. I did like most small businesses do and I just got started and at some point realized my company was lacking identity and a theme. Too many questions came from the prospects that I would call on and had no real idea what we did. I first took the position that they were just clueless but after it happened over and over again, I decided that I was the clueless one and something had to be done.

One day I called around and spoke to a ton of web designers. I picked their brains and gathered as much information as I could draw from them. I had always been good in marketing and understood I was not doing all that I could, but finally realized it was a complete picture that I was missing. I needed to pull it all together. Our service was great and we had a lot going for us but far too many people questioned too much about our identity. Just as I am telling you now, I had to go to work and do my homework. I was a student of what I wanted to learn and was passionate about creating a complete identity. I spent months doing it since we had been up and running for several years. I broke a cardinal rule of building a business. I failed to properly plan and build my business the right way.

A business needs to have a clear theme and message because if you don't, you will spend your whole time explaining it to people. You certainly could spend your time that way but I would suggest spelling it out upfront and then use your time in other ways to build your business. At the end of the day, I finally got it right and my business opened up like never before.

4.1. Using the Best Words

We certainly have tried to make it clear how important an image is, but now we need to take a serious look at the words that make up your brand as well. If an image says a thousand words then what do the actual words say? I'm sure you have heard this before; choose your words wisely. You will be judged by your commandment for the English language or whatever language you might speak. This is not a time to be shy. You must create a fine balance of being excited about your brand and under promising and over delivering. Too much confidence and you will be held to an impossible standard, but if you are not excited about what you do, neither will anyone else.

The words that you can use on your website or social media need to be words that tell a story about who your company is and what it can do for people. Watch getting yourself into legal trouble. Use accurate words that give the prospect an understanding on your company's products or services and why you are the best choice for the prospect. Write the words just like you would like to see if you were searching for a company that does what you do. You must spell out benefits and show value in your offering. Be the best provider of a service and talk about testimonials others have given you. Using the right words will help others identify with you and connect with you.

The right words on line has to be done in two ways in order for you to accomplish clean branding all the while you get your website indexed. You need intelligently written words that brand your company and get people to want to buy from you. You also need search engines to find you and have you show up in results when people do a search for what you offer. The reason I bring this up is because SEO copy is not always the cleanest and well written grammar as traditional writing should be. SEO copy is written in a way that the search engines understand and I would suggest that you learn how to accomplish both. You never want to put a form of writing on line that is going to embarrass you. If you have someone else write SEO copy for you, make sure they understand how to make it sound intelligent. This is a craft and not everyone can do this.

Your writing does not always have to be hard core business related. Writing about causes, human interest, a charity you support or other types of interest that you have also helps to brand your company. Remember, people like to buy from people they know, like and trust. People will feel like they know you more when you brand yourself as something more than just a clerk or all business minded of a person. Let them see another side of you and those who work for you. You will be surprised how powerful this can be for you. Tell your story, get prospects excited about you and show them more than one side of your company and the results will be better than you ever imagined.

What if you are not a great writer? Hire someone as there are plenty of ways to get your words out. If you cannot afford to hire a writer then make sure your words are free from bad grammar and express what you desire to the best of your ability. I would bet that if you keep it simple and just have virtual conversations with people, you will do a fine job of representing your company! You know what your company is all about and you are in the best position of laying it out. Even if you hired someone to write you will still be the one to spell it out for the writer. Have confidence in what you know.

4.2. Managing Your Reputation

When we are talking about building a reputation on line these days, we are not just talking about the reputation that you are putting out. Others will try and brand you as well and in a negative light. This is what we call reputation management and it is important that you always keep an eye out for these situations as they will arise from time to time. Some of these people will try and cause harm to be malicious or while others are trying to get your attention in the hope that you will respond in a positive way. These situations can be a shining moment for you either way. Do not shrink from these remarks and postings.

Make sure that you carefully respond as this will tell others about your brand and they will show up in search. When others look to do business with you, you do not want to lose potential business because of poor responses and bad customer service.

What does a comment or two mean about your brand? Generally does not necessarily mean that you are doing the wrong thing but if you have five, ten or 20 plus then maybe your brand is in deep trouble. Maybe you believe that you are doing right when you are actually alienating your customers and providing a poor product or service. Maybe you are really being a dishonest business trying to fool many or maybe you just don't have what it takes yet to run a business. No matter what the case is you will need to regroup quickly and repair your reputation because with the way online works today, you will certainly suffer if you do not. Both good and bad things spread like wildfire quickly online and you will be under a microscope quick if you do not manage your reputation online.

I am asked all the time if comments should always be responded to and as emphatically and as quickly as I can I respond with a stern no!

Let me explain why so that you will better understand. Some comments where the customer is frustrated and not getting the response they desire, you will need to respond and figure out a way to turn around a bad situation. How you will need to determine if you should respond or not will determine some observation and investigation. See what you can find on the site they have reported you on. Have they left other comments before? Are they rational and level headed comments or do they scream out of control? Do they use curse words and abusive tones? If this seems like a sincere cry for help then see what you can do.

What do you do if these comments are attacks on your brand for the intent of causing you harm? Do not respond because the person who left them will win in more ways than one. The first thing is that a lot of these sites have a lot of activity on them and therefore they are usually strong online. They come up in search engines easily and the more responses that occur, the more likely they will show up under the key words that are chosen. The strongest keyword being used would be your business name and then your personal name will be next.

You might be tempted to want to fire back and defend yourself, but the more you react to these types of people and comments, the more harm it will cause your company. They are waiting and hoping that you will respond to them so that they will get more strength against you. They will work in teams to work against you.

Let me point out to you that these types of online character assassination people are not worth all the muscle and time you will have to spend to fight them off. They have alternative motives in what they are doing and they will waste your valuable time and resources. You do not need to fight this online evil head on. I will give you an idea of what can be done and then if you want to know more keep an eye out for another book coming out called Reputation Management written by me (Robert Kintigh). I will go into more detail how to deal with all of this should it occur.

There are several ways to deal with and remove both negative and positive reputation postings about you and your company. The negative and mean postings we will not respond too. You can try to write these people and see if they would be willing to remove the negative comment but if they are truly being nasty then you shouldn't even bother to contact them.

So what should you do then? How will you deal with the ramifications of these negative postings online? The best way to deal with negative postings about your company is to have them pushed down with other searches. What marketing companies do for their clients is create a bunch of articles, videos, press releases and more that are stronger that what is being reported to online. Every site on the internet has strength to it and when one site is reporting something about you or shows up in search, you need to find something that is stronger to push it down. Create enough postings online with more strength and you can push down anything. At minimum, you will want to create more stuff about your company so that they have plenty to consider. The truth isn't what others say about you. The truth about your company is the entire sum of everything combined.

There is so much more to learn about reputation management but I believe you are getting the idea. Your brand and reputation is on the line each and every day. If you fail to keep an eye on Google, Bing and Yahoo and do not manage your searches, then you are going to lose business and suffer damage to your brand online like you can never imagine. Take the time to put together a schedule to check out the search engines. You or someone on your team can delegate this.

Reputation management is the new credit report that is both fair and unfair to people and businesses. People are protected by free speech to tell their opinion about their experience with you. Because of this right and protection, these sites will not touch someone's freedom of speech or opinion because it would open them up to a lawsuit. If they do not interject their judgment they are protected as well.

I tell you this so you understand what is at stake here. You need to know the rules if you are going to play the game. You will find that the smarter that you are and the better you run your company, the better your online reputation will be.

4.3. What is Your Message?

The basic idea for your brand is to create a message for your prospects and customers. A brand is a well-crafted message of images and words that will relay to your target audience what you are trying to say. This will happen provided you have a message to tell. A message that is clear in its description creates a call to action and that sets your company in the right light. How do you figure out the message that you want to tell with your brand?

When that one day occurred to you and you wanted to start your own business, why did you want to start your own business and what did you decide your new business would be? Besides the obvious of making money, what did you hope to accomplish with your new business? The best part of owning a business is that you have the ability to help others. You can make a difference in people's lives. This is where I would start when it comes to figuring out what your message should be about. Spend some time and really put some thought into it.

Maybe you need to write a mission statement or even just write a story about your business before it even gets off the ground. Write about the look of the company, the charities it supports, the benefits the employees receive, the value the customer gets from dealing with your organization. You will be surprised when you visualize what your company will be about, how much easier it will be to create a brand that has a clear message. You must first know what the message is going to be so that your prospects and customers will understand the message.

Speak to your target audience with sincerity and honesty. Speak to their hearts and minds and make it clear what you are about. You can create a billion dollar brand even if the balance sheet does not show the numbers. Small business does not have to mean that you have a half done brand. You can do this and create brilliance for your company.

I understand how you may be feeling as you start out on this new venture. Starting a business is a big deal and you may lack confidence at times when it comes to what you are doing. You may think that you should not act like a big business and have too much going on. You may be thinking that you do not need a mission statement because no one will even read it. You may also think that your brand only needs to be a logo and a website and you are not big enough to do too much with your business. You are making a big mistake if you are thinking or saying any of this. You are big enough if you own a business. You are big enough if you serve people and have a team working with you of any size. Do not think small just because you are a small business. Think big and act big at all times.

We all start out with small thinking so I understand if that is where you are at right now. Change your thoughts so that you can change your business. A clearly defined message will take you everywhere that you want to go with your small business.

Now that you have the message figured out that will tell the story of your brand, launch it online and let others get to know who you are and what you are about. You will know when the time is right and will launch full throttle.

4.4. Best Practices in Protecting a Brand

The best practices for protecting a brand is by planning everything ahead of time and then keeping a very close eye on it as time moves on. The planning alone will go a long way in protecting your brand

and the constant monitoring of the brand on line is crucial. What you do today you will be rewarded for down the road.

The next way to protect a brand is by doing trademark registration and a copyright registration. You do this to protect the logo, the name and anything else that is unique to your brand. This can cost you some money but there are ways to make this happen so that you can either save money or protect yourself down the road should someone try and harm your brand by using it. Keep in mind I am not a lawyer and anything I tell you is strictly my opinion and nothing more. Have everything I say checked out or proceed with caution.

One way to protect your brand and prove you came up with the idea first is to publish it. I will throw this one out there first because what I call first use (not necessarily a legal term) is very important if you need to prove you used something first. Publish it on line, in a newspaper or anywhere that you can go back to and show you were using it first.

If you want something that seems to be a better option as far as I am concerned then check out companies like Legal Zoom. I am not endorsing them in any way nor I am getting paid to tell you about them but they are an alternative to paying an attorney to protect your brand. They assist in the filing of trademark and copyright for your business amongst other things like incorporating a business. This is generally cheaper, but still may require the help of an attorney.

Using an attorney to file your registration for trademark or copyright is also a way to go. The costs are not cheap but you will have peace of mind that it should get done right. You might also want to have an attorney on retainer to help when there are issues with people attacking your brand or using it in some way not intended. I am not advocating going and suing everyone by any means, but it is always good to have a third party speak on your behalf to keep anything from getting too emotional or personal.

Make sure that you are running an ethical and clean business to the best of your ability. Just know that no matter how hard you try you will not always do the right thing. Business is tough and you will make mistakes. Do your best to clean up your messes always. Do not ignore trouble or make it worse by being aggressive and rude. I have had to learn this and so should you, now instead of later. Protect your brand by fixing what went wrong and you will still be able to shine bright to your customers.

A strong brand online is graceful and exciting. You will want to present a professional side to everything that you do. Even trouble can be presented in a professional way if you handle the issue intelligently and calmly. Do your best to protect your brand on line and it will pay you back a thousand fold!

5. What a Website Says about Your Brand?

If you are just starting your business and haven't created a website yet, I hope to give you some good advice that you will use or consider. If you are already in business and you have a website up and it is giving off the wrong impression then you need to remove it and correct it before it furthers the damage. A web design and SEO expert can take a look at some important elements of your website, how it should look, how it should function, what it should have included in it and the priorities of it.

A website should say that you have a strong brand that is intelligently done and admired by its visitors. You are not going to create the world's best website ever seen. A good website is given a positive nod and then is moved on from and gets a return in the future. A Bad website is passed by quickly and no one ever returns again to it. At best you will get a great job and a return visit. If there ever was a world's best website it might go to Amazon or Facebook but beyond that there is no more room for an awe striking site. They serve a purposeful function and extend your brand.

When you have a website designed, keep in mind that the most information is placed where we call above the fold. This is the area that pulls up and is displayed on your monitor without scrolling. You will want your logo proudly displayed with a sharp look. Make sure that it is done in high resolution. Make sure the lines are crisp and that the colors look vibrant. You want to make sure that everything that is displayed above the fold is what you want people to see first about your brand.

The home page is the most important as well as your about page. Take time to think about what you want people to know most about your company. Give them the best look at your brand and the most important information they need to know about you. Everything needs to be clearly spelled out and there should be a way for visitors to clearly communicate with you. Give your users the best experience possible and do not frustrate them. Put your phone number everywhere as well as an email and map information.

If you have a mobile app, the front page above the fold would be the best place to display how to download your app. Any information that you put on the first page needs to be professionally done. Do not just place things on their randomly. A good website blends and looks like it all belongs together. I also do not suggest putting too much on any one page including using drop down menus. Drop down menus make the page overwhelming users. You are going for a great user experience and too much information drives most people crazy!

A website can say different things about your company and brand; the first being that you care, you are professional, organized, and you get it or the second being that your brand is cheap, disorganized and low class. A website needs to be a great piece of marketing that shows off your brand and creates admirers. If you do not plan your website then you will surely pay for the results. Like everything we have laid out in this book you will need to plan before you execute. Do not just throw pieces together and launch it to the world. Your critiques are waiting for you to slip up and your competition will love your lack of care if you do not plan. Again, do your research so that your brand will represent you in a way that will make you proud.

Lastly, attach all of your social media to your site using attractive icons that make it easy for users to connect. Be sure to design all of your social media to look like your website as you know by now that branding is everything. Keep a consistent look throughout all of your offerings. Most sites will allow you to use graphics or layouts for your back grounds.

5.1. What Does Google Have Figured Out?

You may or may not understand everything to do with Google, but Google has a lot figured out that you can learn from. First and foremost Google is smart enough to understand one very important thing; Google will protect its brand at all cost because their brand is worth a lot. Let me tell you a story about Google that I heard. It is my version, but it is as close to the truth as I know it. The reason I tell you this story is that you have to understand how valuable your brand and name is and what you should do to protect it.

The Google story goes like this: For a long time now, there are these SEO companies who would sell to small businesses and promise them first page listings on Google. They would run AdSense campaigns and create an ad and then charge the companies for these services. Most small businesses really do not understand how Google AdSense works or search engines and such. Needless to say that it is pretty easy to speak technical with business owners and they would not understand a word you would say. Unfortunately a lot of SEO companies know this. There are also plenty of ethical companies so I am not picking on everyone.

Well Google being the smart company they are realized some very important things happening. First, they noticed medium and large companies would spend money on the Google ads and understood their power. Where there was untapped Gold was with the 40 million small businesses of the world and they were not taking advantage of utilizing Google and the power of their AdSense. Google began to check into things to see what it would take to better educate the small businesses so they could get more of them to advertise with Google.

What they found was that when small businesses would finally take a chance and try out Google ads, they often went through these SEO companies and most of the time it was a disaster. A few of the companies would really do well because they would contract with a great company and get the results that they expected. The rest would spend all kinds of money and get nowhere. Google might have said oh well that is just the way it goes but as always Google went further and wanted to get this figured out.

They started to ask questions and poke around and what they heard was very disturbing. When the small businesses would not get the results that they wanted they would not blame the SEO company. What they would say is, "This Google stuff doesn't work!" Google said wait, these campaigns do work and we need to figure out why they are having such poor results. What they found out was that the SEO companies would charge big money and very little was going towards the campaign. They might charge a thousand dollars a month to the small business but only three hundred dollars might actually go to the campaign. This is very disproportional to what should be happening. Google said enough as they want to protect their good name and so they implemented a policy as to what could be charged for these services.

Imagine if you had enough sense to go that far with your brand. I know you have way too much to do but if Google thinks this kind of thing is a high priority then maybe you should as well. Take no chances of others hurting your good name. Go the extra mile and if something is not right then investigate further and get to the bottom of it!

5.2. What Are Your Employees Posting on Social Media?

As an employer you will want to write policy and control what your employees do on Facebook especially if they are a public figure for your company or if they use your name on their profile. If they talk about where they work, post pictures from the office or anything else, you will want to have policy in place ahead of time to ensure that there is no backlash towards your brand. Yes it is their Facebook, but you have the right to install policy as a condition of employment or continued employment to control what happens publicly with your people.

Nothing can harm a company's image more than having your people on line doing things that may not match up to your company image. They may be posting pictures of themselves drinking every night and partying while saying they work at a health food company or a health and Fitness studio. What if you were a doctor's office? While they are drinking and partying, they are also stuffing fast food into their mouth, and peeling the banana on camera. All the while they show that they work at XYZ Health & Fitness. Maybe you own a car lot with nice cars and your employees are all driving around in beater cars and always posting pictures on Facebook. What would this do for your image?

Is this a problem with all of your employees? Probably not as we know the research shows is that the age group from 18-30 is your biggest problem. If you are going to enforce policy though, you will need to write a blanket policy, not just aged based. You will need to control it across the board. This policy has to be for everyone at your firm or organization.

Maybe pictures are not the problem but the people who work for you are always complaining about their job or posting status updates while at work about how they can't wait to leave their work place at five o'clock! None of this paints a very good picture about your company or brand and your employees are not realizing the effect that they are or could be having on your brand. You will need to do some coaching and training and lay out policy on what is acceptable when it comes to social media.

What people do in their personal life is not necessarily all personal and if the public knows they work for you then you will need to take an active role in monitoring and managing social media. These younger adults have no concept or shame for that fact of what should be on Facebook. The older generation has some guilt as well but as of right now, they have not grown up in this age of social media but as time moves on it will become a problem.

Social media should be encouraged to spread goodness about the company and perhaps you can put on classes about how your employees can help with the company on line using their own profiles. Maybe you can start some kind of reward program for spreading positive updates about the company and make it an incentive program. Maybe you can have contests and spell out what you are looking to have on line or reward employees for handling themselves well on line.

No matter what you decide, keep an eye on everyone who works for you on line. Make sure you check on a regular basis. Before you hire, do a search on line and see what you find. You might be very surprised as to what you can learn just by doing this before you say yes to bring them on board.

5.3. Why Use the Voice of a Blog?

Have you figured out yet what is the purpose of a blog yet? Have you even considered writing a blog for your company? How will your brand benefit from the voice of a blog? People write blogs for many things and no matter why you write a blog there are many things to celebrate about the experience and exercise as a blog has a voice like no other and your company can benefit from it when it is done well. Why use the voice of a blog? The answer is simple; because it gives your company a chance to explain everything that it would like people to know about it. A blog is a perfect branding tool for laying out all of the pieces to your company. Pictures are great for visual look and videos do a great job visually, but a blog will do all of that and then some and help you to express what your company is all about.

How do you get started and what should you start to talk about? What is the average size of each article and who is your target audience? I am sure that you have questions especially if you have never utilized a blog. I was where you are at if this is the case and will provide a little hand holding because for branding yourself on line, a blog is a fabulous tool for many reasons. I cannot lay everything out here, but I will give you a great start and overview and I hope to encourage you to have a blog designed and started as soon as possible.

How do you start a blog? There are many ways to set up a blog and there are some technicalities to work out, but one of the most popular is setting up a Wordpress blog. This can be done either at www.wordpress.com which will host your blog for you, but has some restrictions as to what you can write about and post. A truly professional set up with Wordpress is to host it yourself. This is the best way to go because you can post what you want without any restrictions. You will need to contact someone if you do not understand what I am saying. What I am suggesting to you is to set up Wordpress on your own hosting so keep that in mind.

Where you should start the conversation is by setting up the foundation for who your company is, how it was founded and why and what you provide. Tell small stories at a time filled with plenty of keywords. Keywords are words that people might use to search for what you do or who you are. You want to carry on a story long term that tells the story of what your brand is all about. A blog can be a very powerful marketing tool when you learn to write without selling. The key is to put out useful information and added value to your readers.

The average size of each article should be no less than about 350-400 words and no more than about a page full. Really how much you write should be tied in with how frequent that you will be writing. The more you write, the less you can post. The least amount that you write should be done more often, meaning 350 words should be written more often than articles that have 1000 words. Your target audience should be determined each time that you write. With smaller articles you may be able to really target in on different audiences for your articles. Avoid general articles as they tend to draw less of a search.

The time to get blogging is now and I hope we have given you a place to start so you can continue to extend your brand on line. Give your business a voice and a blog is a way

6. Video Branding 101

If a picture says a thousand words then a video will say the rest needed! Video has become a standard for branding and dominating search on line and a company cannot survive on line without it. It was not that long ago that video was very difficult to master on line and the everyday use of it was reserved for highly technical videographers and web masters. Today that has all changed and businesses have discovered one of the most powerful ways to brand their company! In this section of the book we are going to talk about video as an on line branding tool and some basics that will help you to leverage video for your business.

Why do you think video is such a great tool for branding and communicating on line? From a sales perspective, people buy from those they know, like and trust. With the use of video you have a chance to have you and your company's face shown. If people cannot stand right in front of you and hear it straight from your mouth then video is the next best thing. Not a fan of being on camera? There are many ways to leverage video and you do not even have to get on camera all too often. I do suggest though showing your face every once in a while. Your worse video is better than not showing your customers and prospects who you are and what you look like to include others who are a part of your business.

Videos should be created very similar to the blog articles. Keep them short and distributed very often. I would not however create 20-40 minute videos as you will not hold the attention of the people watching them. People like to watch videos that are short and to the point. People love to learn new things from videos so anything that you can teach them is a plus for you. Show the value in dealing with your company which is more than possible with video.

How do you get started leveraging video to build your brand on line? The types of videos you can create or pay someone to create are videos of you talking in front of a video camera about your business. You can make them or have someone else in the company who is comfortable in front of the camera. There are really only two types of videos on the internet that are effective. The first one is a Hollywood production and the second one is a down to earth, real video. If you do not make one of these two videos then what you will end up with is a cheesy video that looks like you are trying to be more than you are. You do not have to create Hollywood productions 99% of the time.

The other types of videos to use are either teaser videos, commercial type videos, PowerPoint videos and high end productions. No matter what you decide make sure you are putting your best foot forward. A video should extend your brand and has the ability to do so by being distributed over and over again. You can get a lot of leverage out of each and every video that your company produces so make sure they are quality.

What you will do with your videos is distribute them on line to video sites, social media sites, websites, blogs, classified sites and more. Do a search on line and you will find a ton of video sites more than just YouTube. There are literally thousands of places to post your video and write something about it to let people discover your brand. Video has a lot of strength in search engines.

6.1. Will Your Brand Ever Be Truly Complete?

If you ever get to that point where you think that your brand is complete then you are probably in trouble. Your job will always be to constant refine and make your brand better on line. You will constantly have to work on extended your brand and helping it to reach further. You will need to fix things at time and clean up situations.

Business is always changing and on line it is changing even faster. Theoretically, your brand will never truly be complete. What you will be is at a state of professionalism that will make you proud to have built a brand that is respectable. If you get to a point where your brand is strong then you will enjoy the profits of your hard work.

Some of the stuff I written in this book is what I would call elementary and some of it is advanced. I wrote all of this about branding because I know the majority of the people in this world have a long way to go when it comes to branding on line. This information on branding is meant to either help you begin to properly brand your company on line or will help you to repair it or extend further.

Missing out on the power of branding your company on line in the right way is overlooked. Most people equate branding as something only big corporations do. Most small businesses fail to plan most of their business and branding is one of those elements that are greatly overlooked.

You know about branding a lot more than you think as you have been around it your whole life. McDonalds, UPS, Microsoft, Google, Oprah Winfrey, Tony Robins, Verizon and more have shown you great ways to brand your company. All you really have to do is spend time thinking about what you really like about these brands or theirs and then invent your own version.

You might ask yourself now that you are at the end of this section on branding if you really have what it takes to create an award winning brand? Will people really care about something that you create and put together? What I would ask you if I could is what the alternative is? Do you just start a company and do whatever to it and get whatever results? Maybe even worse would be to doubt yourself and never take a step forward towards your dreams. Let me assure you that you can do this and create an incredible brand. Most consumers really are just looking for an honest company to deal with. This is the easiest place to start. Then start conversations and build relationships so people will want to engage with you on line.

We have come to that point where you now need to get to work on your brand. What I have provided to you will get you on the road to where you really want to be. I wish you all the best and hope that I have provided value to you. If you would like to contact me or my internet marketing firm then you will find that on the next page. Please let me know how it is going with your brand and if what I have provided to you makes a difference. Our goal is to help as many small businesses build a strong company and live the life they desire.

If your brand is not top priority to you then it will never be top priority to your customers! Only you can give your company the life it hungers for. Take charge of your business and everything that goes with it and you will end up the best place possible.

7. Sales Tips 101 - The Beginning

For over twenty two years I have made a great living in the highest paid profession in the world. I have enjoyed a lifestyle that so many people would love to have. I am not bragging to you, but I am trying to impress upon you that if you have picked up this book because you want to be better as a salesperson or if you are considering switching careers and you are considering a career in sales, I want to help you achieve everything that you want and then some. Sales Tips 101 for Future Top Salespeople is a wonderful story about the greatest profession in the world.

I really started my sales career as a child and learned at a young age that the secret to being a great salesperson is not giving up, not giving in and that attitude determines everything. I wanted to write a book that would help up and coming sales people learn the secrets of what I had to share.

As we move on throughout the chapters you will learn some of my best secrets that have created a ton of sales and some great relationships. I am hoping to deliver a look at the process of sales that can be accomplished as something that should be second nature to you. Creating sales is like creating conversations, identifying needs, wants and pains and helping people with what they want and need.

To be great as a sales person, you need to make every day a fun game that you plan out and learn how to hit your goals. I will teach you some very special mental aspects of sales and how you can learn to overcome even the most challenging days. Every day will not always be smooth and in fact some days will down right be tough and hard to deal with.

Why do so many people shrink when they see the sales person come through their front door? Should you ignore the sign on the wall that says no soliciting? How do you get the person at the front desk to help you? I know you have many questions and are not always sure if you are doing the right thing. We take a look at all of these situations and dispel some ideas that might have you hung up.

Achieving great sales and becoming successful as a salesperson takes the right mindset and learning how to carry yourself is extremely important to learn. You need to know what you are doing is what is going to make you successful and will help you to push doubt out of your mind because this is very important.

Over the years I have sold millions upon millions of dollars of products and services. Like most people I started out at the beginning making all kinds of mistakes and as I have gone along in my sales career, I continue to make a lot of mistakes. You will never have it all down but as a professional salesperson you will always work on your game. I have never let down in my sales career and if you are smart you will not either. If today is day one you have a lot to learn.

If you are a veteran with many years, then you have a lot to learn. As salespeople we must have a deep seated thirst for learning because the career we have chosen involves two major aspects; one is we deal with people and two because we deal with people what we do is very psychological. This makes what you do very difficult but very achievable as for over 100 years not much really has changed when it comes to people and getting them to buy!

Why you want to read this book is because we have pulled together resources for the newbie or the veteran. We discuss some of the most powerful techniques and strategies. We help you develop your winning mindset and how to set yourself up to succeed. This book will give you the straight forward information that you need to quickly become a top salesperson in your company.

Have ever figured out yet that people hate to be sold to but they love to buy? If this is the case what part do you play in the sales process? What can you do to help them to decide to buy from you? Do not fool yourself just because people love to buy and hate to be sold to. You are one of the most important pieces in the sales process. We will lay out the foundation as to what your duties are in the sales process and how you can be the best possible to assist the prospect in the buying process.

Let's get ready to dig in and take notes as we are going to get you on the road to your new riches. I want to mention something before we get moving here and that is no matter if you are new or a veteran, you always have the chance to stop and restart as a sales professional. What I mean is that as you are moving about your day to day duties and you are laser focused, you will often get off track. One of the things I did not learn until later in life is that you have to stop every once in a while to gain clarity and get back to where you should be.

So on with the show and let's help you to become the future top sales person at your company. I want to help you be the best and hit your goals. Let's turn some heads and show you why your choice of being a top sales person is going to be life changing!

7.1. Where Sales Begin?

If we are going to get ourselves in the right position to be a future top sales person, don't you think that we should fully understand the sales process and where sales begin? I think that is exactly where we should start and so let's take a look at where sales begin and what all is involved in the sales process. I encourage you to take notes every step of the way and analyze everything we are talking about. Take nothing for granted as we begin to dive into this exciting topic that I love to teach and talk about.

Where do sales begin? The answer is simple; when people have a need, want or pain. Let's take a look at each one of these and then discuss the sales cycle that is involved to move them to where they want to buy from you. If you are going to be a professional in the sales process then we understand that people love to buy and hate to be sold. Let's look at how you can accomplish this and why their needs, wants and pains are the key to making that happen for you.

People will always buy what they need and derive survival pleasure and have only great emotion tied to buying something they need if they have been without for an extended period of time. Human nature has shown over and over again that needs are important but not until they are met. What I mean is that if we need food and water, we will go about filing those needs but we do not shed a tear as long as it happens. Once it stops happening we will get very emotional until we get it again and then it is back to business as usual.

So if people's needs are not very emotionally driven then how do we compel people to buy from us if we sell water or food or clothing or other needs that a person must have? In this area of sales as I have stated above, unless they are in desperate need of their want there is no high demand and so you will have to work on two things and really a third as well to get them to buy. One is price which is a tough one to sell on as people who buy on price are high maintenance generally. The second is on relationship and that is a long term strategy. The last is on service and quality. When people buy on needs they leave very little room for professionalism when it comes to being a sales person.

The good news is they still have choices to get their needs from, but the bad news is there are very little factors that will affect much change. If all things are equal then price and location (or convenience) will generally win out.

Next is people's wants. The good news about people's wants is that when people have one want, it will turn into two wants which will turn into three wants as they get more money. We have seen this in many cases from televisions to DVD players to cars and electronics. In America this is what fuels our economy.

When people buy what they want, this is called discretionary spending. What this means is that when they have the money and can afford to spend it, they spend it. When the economy is good, you have a great chance of gaining their business even when you are marginal as a sales person. When the economy tightens up, you must be at the top of your game or close to it as they are going to be very choosy as to where they get there wants from. You have a great chance of showing them value and attributes of what you have.

You also can build relationships to gain the sale, educate people with what is out there, and build loyalty and more. Wants have great flexibility in them and will allow you to use what you know as a sales person to gain sales. The down fall to wants besides a bad economy is that they rank second to a powerful motive next to pains. They also are a luxury item so even though they give more flexibility they lack the idea of must have.

The top motivated buyer is a person with pains. A person with a pain will give anything to get rid of the pain. Think of this buyer like a person on fire who will pay anything for your bucket of water. Price does not matter or location or sometimes even how good of a sales person you are. This is a time however to shine and really set the marketplace with who you are as a sales person. Pains give you the best light to shine in with the prospect.

A pain is defined in different ways for different people and understanding people's pains are essential to your success. The reason that I believe this is because if you want to standout, have people buy from you and create long term sales then you will figure out people's pains and then you will help solve them. To take this a step further you will have to treat everyone like an individual and spend at least a few minutes and figure out who is in front of you and what is their biggest problem. Once that is completed then you need to figure out if what you have can alleviate their pain. If the answer is yes then you are in the driver's seat.

Do you want to know some of the pains that people have so that you can gain understanding of what I am talking about? I am sure by now I am at least grabbing your attention as you may have never heard this concept before and I assure you that what I am talking about is very real. I will give you some real examples of people's pains after I tell you about a sales position I held at a company called Tradesmen International out of Cleveland Ohio.

I was hired to help open an office in Seattle Washington and the concept was fairly simple to understand. We would hire labor (electricians, construction workers, plumbers, welders, etc.) and then we would lease them out to Contractors, power plants, building owners, etc. Two other salesmen were hired when I was with each of us having our territory. We would get in front of prospects and promote our labor force. In the construction industry and other industries that are similar, the problem or pain that they have is that they either have too much labor or not enough as rarely do they have just the right amount. Our job was to take out the ups and downs of their labor pool as this concept or pain was taught to us by our company.

I am sure that is where at best the other two sales people lived that opened that office with me as I would have out the majority of the labor force most of the time. This pain is a good place to start but ultimately there were additional pains that went with this one and it was my job to uncover them. Again, this is an individual problem and therefore I had to attack it that way. I would get to know my prospects and customers and would always look for ways to help them with their pains.

Without being too graphic, what would you be willing to do if you had a knife jabbed into your leg to remove the pain? What if you had not eaten in 2 weeks? What would you be willing to do for food?

What if you have been in the snow for a week lost and your toes were getting frost bitten? What would you be willing to do to get rid of the pain? Now imagine in all of these scenarios I came along and fixed your pains? What would my worth be to you?

My sales position at Tradesmen International was a series of house calls with my "patients." No, I was not a real doctor of medicine but I was a real doctor of fixing pains for my clients and prospects. Business pains are just as excruciating to them as the knife scenario or the lack of food example with the other people. Do not get confused because a knife is physical pain and not having enough labor is not.

To a business man or project manager, these pains are just as hurtful and if you are looking for the physical pain side to it then watch as stress sets in on a person. Worry tends to cause lack of sleep as well as not getting home until 10:00 p.m. at night from a pain like this. What would you be worth if you could solve these issues?

I would spend my days going from one client to another just looking for ways to help and fix their pains. It was like a game that I had fun with all day long and it paid off very quickly. In no time I had generated a million dollars in sales and my clients were very happy with me. I would bring them in from time to time as we grew and I would let them talk to others in the office to give them the feel that they had for what I was doing different. My clients always talked about how I was there to help and solve problems. They never felt like I was there to sell anything! Remember what I had said in my introduction? People love to buy but they hate to be sold anything!

Business owners, managers, foremen, leaders, property managers and everyone else who is involved in running a business have all kinds of pains on a daily basis and if you are willing to look for them and help them get rid of them, then you will stand out and your pay will reflect your efforts.

Pains to look for as you go about your day are: too much work not enough time to complete it. Need specific type of skilled employee or is frustrated with a current provider. Their current space they are in is too small or their car is falling apart. This is just a generic list of ideas but I hope they get you paying attention as there are millions to encounter. Pay attention, take notes and ask lots of high-gain questions. Most people cannot help themselves but to talk about what is ailing them. Questions will get you where you need to be.

As we continue on with our journey to be a top sales person, keep in mind that helping people with their pains are very profitable. I am not asking you to prey on people with issues but I am setting you up to help people with problems they currently possess. You are going to see people that will want to buy from you and will remain loyal to you in your quest for success!

7.2. The Greatest Elements of a Sales Person

The greatest elements that a sales person can obtain and possess are elements that are mostly common sense in nature. There really is little magic as some might have you to believe. Do not get me wrong as it seems like magic when you understand how it all works but the truth is there is a lot of common sense at work.

The first element to focus on is to be a great listener is you are going to be a great sales person! Listening is a fine art and should be worked on from day one. You might be sitting there saying that you are a good listener and you may be right. There is a big difference though when it comes to listening to prospects and strangers. It is easier to listen to people you know and may find interesting but let's face it, some of the prospects that you will come across will be really boring.

The other part to being a good listener in the sales process is to understand what to listen for and what things mean when the prospect or customer talks about it. For instance, I have a mobile app business that is prime for small business and when It sit down with a small business and I get them to talk about themselves, I listen for words like the economy is tough or I can't seem to get any leads off of my website or I need more prospects. This is a clear sign for me to show them how to fix this problem with my mobile apps for sale. Attentive listening during the sales process means to listen for the clues from the prospect and then to know the questions to ask to help them to buy from you.

Which brings me to the next important element of a top sales person is the ability to question. When you learn the art of listening to your prospects and customers you then need to learn how to question. We need open ended questions that will get them to speak freely and tell us what we need to know in order to be able to present our option to help with their pains.

You have to be patient when you are listening and you have to have the ability to think while they are telling you all that you need to know. It may seem tough but after a while it will become second nature. All you need to do is ask simple questions while you are in the sales process. You will have to work on the questions depending on what you are selling but if you listen well and have a game plan, and then the questions will guide you to where you need to be.

The next important element is formulating a game plan. The off the cuff type of sales person is a sales person who is going nowhere. A game plan will give you guidance and understanding. It will force you to formulate questions and figure out where you are taking the relationship with each prospect you get in front of. A game plan is what professionals do when it comes to the sales process. They understand that a game plan is essential to knowing where they are going much like an airplane pilot.

The last of the important elements top sales people need to possess is the element of care. Care is a very important element as it should make sure that you do all of the elements with the highest regard for your profession. Care should drive you to make sure that you actually care about your prospects and clients. Care may be the most important element of all of the elements.

7.3. The Basic Ideas of Creating Sales

How do you create sales when you are working with clients or prospects? This can happen in many ways but I will give you an idea how we did it when I owned my Handyman Maintenance business. My hope is that I can give you real live examples and then you will be able to figure out what applies to your industry.

My company sent out repair men and women to fix problems at homes and commercial property like doors and windows and cabinets and such. They were there usually because the customer needed some new base boards, but I trained everyone to keep their eyes open while they were on people's property. I taught them to look at lights, door bells, windows, roofs, flooring, etc. and if they would see something else broken, they would simply ask the property owner if they would like an estimate on whatever else was noticeable. This is a simple example of how to create sales.

What do you sell? What kind of sales do you think you could create? Maybe you are not a handyman/woman company but instead you sell cleaning products. Ask to use the restroom and see how their fixtures are holding up. There are so many scenarios how you can create sales and increase sales.

The basics of creating sales are being proactive with your clients and prospects. For instance you can send an email or postcard once a month reminding them about weather change or maybe school is starting up soon and suggest some kind of special. Your job is to wake up your clients sometimes and put a bug in their ear or remind them of what can be done in advance.

You never have to pressure people. What you can do is constantly send suggestions to them and ask questions to spark their memory of what they might need. Do not become pushy or a nuisance but if you are going to be a professional then you will keep notes on your customers and continue to help to solve pains for them.

In order to create sales your customers and prospects need to know clearly what you do. Let me tell you about a true story that happened to me once when I ran my maintenance and construction business. It taught me a lesson I thought I had already learned.

For many years I operated a handyman business of sorts. Our company did pretty much everything repair, remodel and building but I liked to classify my company more of a handyman company than anything else because it gave me several advantages. Amongst many of the clients we had, we did a lot of work for the retail industry. Most retailers use management companies to handle all of the repair work they need. We had one particular client who we did a lot of work for but it paled in comparison to what we would end up getting from them.

One day one of my contacts called me from their company and asked if we did some very basic work. I was shocked he was asking me if we did that kind of work so I asked him why he didn't know all of the things we did. I told him we did painting and carpentry, flooring, tile work, doors, windows and on and on. He was shocked as all he thought we did was a little drywall repair, some cleanup work and small handyman type stuff. We increased our business with that company by 1000% over night! I learned a very valuable lesson I thought I had already learned previous and that is keep the conversations continually going so that your customers are well informed of everything that you do.

Imagine had I had the conversation earlier how many sales I could have realized. I would love to tell you that what I just told you is something advanced in the sales process but it really is basic. I just needed a reminder. Sometimes when we get busy making sales we often miss some of the easiest and most basic ones. We have to remain vigilant in creating basic sales all the time.

7.4. From Cold Call to Warm Lead

Every relationship starts out as a cold call at some point. I am always being asked what do when I run out of my warm market. The answer is simple and that is you should be working on new relationships and turn the cold into a warm one.

The game of sales is a continuous process and if you do not work the complete process then you will always hit a flat period and turning cold calls into warm leads will be one of them. Think about this for a moment; you go on 5-10 calls a day and half of those are warm leads. If you do not continue to find new relationships and prospects and convert them into some kind of relationships, then all you will have are strangers who have no interest in knowing you or understanding you. What I mean is that as sales people we always need to be looking for new people to build relationships with or risk stalling out your sales.

Have you heard of the term to *fill your pipeline*? I do not know the origination or the true meaning but the idea is that in order for great pressure to occur in a pipe you have to fill it full of tons of water first. Then if the pressure is great enough the pipe will burst and flood everything. This pipeline of yours is about people and relationships.

At the end of the day, creating outrageous sales and hitting your quotas is a numbers game. Even a mediocre salesperson will have great results if they increase their numbers. What are the numbers? The numbers are how many people you get in front of and present to. How many doors you walk into and how many phone calls you make. How many relationships you build and how many people you help. Increase any of these numbers and your pay check number will increase.

One of the best ways to turn cold calls into warm is by learning how to help people and that does not always mean selling them something. Nominate their business for an award or help them with their can food drive they are putting on. Get them some free press or refer them to someone who can help them. You are trying to get noticed and this is an excellent way to get noticed.

One day I was in a training class and the instructor was going around the room playing a word association game. She said when I point to you I want you to say the first thing that comes to your mind. The word she used was sales person and when she pointed to me I said, "Outsiders." She was passing by people quickly after they said their thoughts but with me she stopped and quickly came back to me. Why do you say that? I said simple, most salespeople are like outsiders and no one wants to let them in. My job is to become an insider!

Doesn't this make complete sense? When you first meet a prospect, are you not an outsider? Isn't the trick to figure out how to become an insider? Think of it this way, if I came to your house and I knocked on the door, would you open up the door and let me right in? Probably not, as we do not know each other as well as trust each other. Somehow people go to office buildings and walk right in and think they will be received with open arms. You are a stranger with no relationship and these prospects are trying to decide right now if they should take time with you to get to know you. Turn cold calls into warm calls and you will quickly change your whole world!

Robert D. Kintigh

8. Top 10 Things You Should Do as a Top Salesperson

I know of some athletes who listen to dance music and or upbeat music while they stretch and get prepared for a game. They get their mind ready to get moving at top speed and because of that they are working on focusing in. They have other rituals as well like watching film or reading plays. This is what the top athletes do so what should top sales people do on a daily basis to get ready for their best game?

From the moment I get out of bed, I am going over what I have to accomplish that day. If I have a big presentation to give I am rehearsing it in my mind. If I need to make an important phone call I role play the words I will use. I get my mind ready for the day and week ahead. I mentally work on my pitches and who I want as a client. In the shower is no different as I am mentally preparing. The more you get yourself in character and prime your mind, the better everything will flow.

Before I ever get into my car, I check my planner and see what plan I really have laid out. I never just go anywhere aimlessly. I know where I am going and what I am trying to accomplish. I need to do this or I will just waste windshield time and my paycheck will show it. Have a plan because without a plan you will fail!

So here are the top ten things you should do daily as a top sales person:

#1 - Prepare mentally for your day
#2 - Check your plan to make sure you have a solid one.
#3 - Role play your scripts so they are smooth and fluent
#4 - Review your products or services and become fluent in understanding them.
#5 - Get in front of 5-10 people a day
#6 - Work on Self-improvement daily

#7 - Contact their mentor

#8 - Ask for referrals from clients

#9 - Look at your goals and bench marks and figure out how to blow them up

#10 - Dream bigger everyday

Like any professional athlete, super star, entertainer, singer or salesperson, you have to get yourself mentally prepared to have your best day. Getting up and just going about your duties will give you plain mediocrity and the outcome will be disappointing. These 10 things are a minimum starting point you should be doing every day. Take each one of these a develop them and live by them.

Top salespeople or people who want to be top sales people will do these ten things every day. I know it because I have and I have seen others who have worked for me do them. Others will just pretend or never do them and then will be frustrated when they do not get to where they want to. What I have given you are gems and you should value them. If you want outrageous results and sales then follow the process. Great things will follow just by being vigilant in the process.

8.1. How to Use the Phone for Cold Calling

Cold calling on a phone is not easy these days but I am not sure they have been for a long time. At least since I have been around so how do you get what you need from cold calling? Someone asked me not long ago if cold calling was even worth it? My answer to them was simple for me as I said that cold calling is no different than everything else we do to gain attention and create a sale. If we are good at it we will get a return from it. If we are not good at it then we get what we get. Is cold calling even worth it still? I say yes it is if you are willing to become proficient at it and a professional. Let's take a look at ways to use the phone to your advantage.

The first thing to know about using the phone as a sale tool is that people are on the defensive right away when they even sniff out a solicitor. That is you, a solicitor so make sure you understand that. We do not really want to be a solicitor and what our main goal should be is to turn a cold call into a warm call. When the person on the other side of the phone answers, we need to lower their defenses immediately without wasting their time. I like to start off a lot of times with the question, "how are you doing today?" This is harmless enough and it takes them off guard. The reason is that most weak salespeople try to blast their way through the door or phone if you will.

Never blast at people, always finesse or calm people without being cheesy. I knew a sales person once who used to use the cheesiest lines I have ever heard. He had been using these lines forever when I came across him and thought they had worked well. He would say things like, "wow, you have a very pretty voice." Now, I don't know about you but the first time I heard that it screamed weirdo to me and maybe even creepy. I said to him one day, "why do you use those lines?

He replied back, "Because they work well!"

Here is how I saved this poor guys life one day with one great question and a follow up explanation. I said, "What is the most money you have ever made in one year in sales?" He stated proudly that one year he made $38,000.00. I about had a heart attack because he was so proud.

I went on to explain to him that sales was the highest paid profession in the world and his best year was $38,000.00 and that would put him at the bottom of the ladder in sales in regards to money made in a given year. He was flattened. After he calmed down I explained to him that those lines he was using were not very intellectual, professional or a great way to create a relationship. He just did not know any better and explained to me that his grandfather used lines like that when he was in sales. I asked how old his grandfather was and he said 89 years old. Those lines might have worked back in the forties and fifties but today is a new ball game. You must use language that is current with the times.

I can happily report to you today that he is making 6 figures and all though I am not totally responsible for it, he still gives me credit today for opening up his mind to better ways to using the phone as he still uses cold calling. Be a professional and try going at people in a different way than everyone else and you can have tremendous success.

The next thing to learn about using the phone for cold calling is always be respectful no matter how you are treated. The reason I say this is because in today's world everyone has caller I.D. and you may have never made it to the point of giving your name, they may already have it on file with their phone system. Never embarrass yourself or your company by losing your cool over the phone and thinking who cares because they don't even know who you are. You will be shocked when they call back and ream you out some more. Always be polite, courteous and professional.

The phone can be a great way to build a micro warm lead. Even if you cannot get to who you want, get to know the person who answers the phone as you may need him or her later if you walk into the office or if someone else answers later. Just knowing Amy's name will help you out a lot of the time later.

When you call back later to their office, act as if you should be calling them and command in a good way the person who you want to speak with. Confidence rules and the better you can learn how to use it the sooner you are going to build a relationship with the next person at the company.

The phone is a great research tool. I call this micro-researching. I have some times called a business I really want to do business with multiple times and see who answers. This will give me an idea of how big they might be, might give me someone who is nicer and more open to help me or give me a person who never answers the phone which can turn out to be huge for me as they may not be on guard at all. Their lack of experience answering the phones can be a blessing so I seize the moment should it happen.

Don't let the phone scare you in any way as it can be a great tool if you are willing to learn to use it. I have never been afraid of using the phone for cold calls as it has always paid off for me in a big way. Like most marketing tools it has it percentage of success rate. You will learn in sales and in marketing that no one thing is a home run. The home run comes in being consistent and utilizing as much as you can manage. A complete offering is where the money is at when it comes to sales and the phone is just one more cog in your wheel house.

Like email, a cold call can be considered Spam of sorts but if done right you can always just ask for forgiveness. There are some laws against it but being a professional should never get you in trouble. What you might seek at times is permission so I love getting business cards or having referrals given to me or a name or something. This is great permission for calling. Also, the internet makes calling these companies okay as well as if they are advertising on line then this is permission as well. This is my interpretation so take it for what it is worth but if they didn't want people to call them then they would not have their phone number all over on line.

If you are honest and polite then you will probably never have any issues. Make sure that you understand etiquette on the phone and you will generally be fine. I can't however say that you will not get some grouches who answer the phone. I call places all the time that should not have people answering their phones. I have employed one or two of these people as well, so just know they are out. Try and see if you can change their mood around in 20 seconds or less and have fun. If not, maybe hang up and try calling back.

8.2. What to do if the Sign Says No Soliciting?

How many times have you walked up to a door and you saw a sign that says no soliciting? What do you do when you see it? Do you freeze or stop dead in your tracks? Do you run for your car in the hopes you were not seen? Maybe you walk in apologetically and ask for forgiveness for intruding. What I propose may surprise you but what I do is put on blinders and I never acknowledge that the sign even exist. You read that right and do not misunderstand me in what I am saying.

So I have been telling you to be professional and polite and never be rude in any way. I have been telling you that we need to build relationships and now all of a sudden I am telling you to walk through doors that say get out unless I have invited you. What can I possible mean by this tactic? How can I possibly be setting you up to succeed when I am waling you right through the door into a den of lions?

Before you get too excited, let me explain why we are going to walk through the door even though it says no soliciting. As a business owner for over 22 years I can tell you that one of the things you are always looking for as a CEO or business owner is resources. This is not just about needing money and in fact other resources are often more valuable. Maybe I have been looking for someone to help write new content or I am tired of the lousy service my bathroom supply company has been delivering but the problem is I am too busy to go hunting for one so I put up with the lousy service. Hopefully I will get lucky and someone brave will walk through the front door even though I have a no soliciting sign up.

Yes I have even been guilty of having one of those signs up but for me it is because I know if you will ignore that sign then I might have someone standing in front of me who deserves to be standing there and therefore you might just be the restroom supply company and representative I have been wanting.

Often times we put up signs to ward away the weak and unworthy and the rest gets a free pass. Do you think I am the only one who thinks this way? Every small business owner if not all business owners, CEO's, middle and top managers are too busy to deal with the masses and we need some way to keep some of the unworthy back. What we all have in common is a need of better resources at all times. *EVERYONE* in these positions always has this issue! I will warn you that if you decide to walk through the door and you are not worthy then you will be whisked away like an annoying alley cat and your efforts will all be for nothing.

What should you be prepared for if you walk through the sign? You need to have your best elevator pitch prepared and ready to launch. This may not necessarily be a sales pitch but an elevator pitch that will actually let you on the elevator. This pitch may have to be for the guy or gal at the front desk. Then you may need another one for whoever might come up front and see you. Be prepared or get ready for some great lessons that may hurt initially. If you are going to be brave enough to walk through the door then take the time to be prepared to make an impression. I am not saying don't do it if you are not ready but you might as well spend time preparing since you are going in.

8.3. Look for Ways to Touch Your Prospects

I know the title may seem a bit weird but what I am talking about is virtual touches so do not get yourself in trouble by petting your prospects. A touch is defined as a reason to get in front of your prospects or clients. You may think that you have them as a client so I do not need to come up with reasons to get in front of them but if you think this way then you are probably either not successful or are doing it without thinking about it.

Over 22 years ago I ran a handyman business and I helped out a local florist with payments who was tight on money by doing the work on her small building in exchange for flowers. At the time I was thinking

I hope I could get some value out of the exchange and had no idea at the time just how powerful those flowers were going to be. In fact truth be told I think I can out better than the florist did.

Since I did not have to worry about the cost I never hesitated to use the flowers. I first started using them almost in a sexiest way and would send them to women only. About 80% of the time I would get thanked profusely and would magically end up with work. That is not even where I made the biggest discovery of the power of touching my clients and prospects. Once I had the sending flowers to women down I started to try and find ways to send flowers to men as well. It took me a while but it became very easy to do so as weird as you might be thinking right now. I sent flowers for happy anniversary, death in the family, birth in the family, not feeling well or a baptism of a child. Magically work would get sent my way.

Once I learned about flowers I learned really that virtual touching or finding ways to get in front of these people could be done in so many ways. Here is something that may surprise you. Let's say that you own an auto repair shop and you are the salesperson for that shop. Your best friend breaks down and doesn't even think to call you but instead takes his car to the guy on the corner closest to his house. He casually brings it up later and you are shocked. Why would this happen do you think? I can tell you how it probably happened and that is although he is your best friend, you have failed to keep your business fresh in his mind and give him a reason to come to you for repairs. He just remembered that the guy on the corner has a sign out front that says 30% off for first time customers.

You continually look for ways to touch clients and prospects so that you can keep what you do fresh in their mind. This may sound silly but here is how the scenario works; they are not ready to buy now and you have no idea when they will be ready to buy. A car breaks down when it feels like breaking down. Your job is to always appear like you are always around one way or another so that when it is time to buy, it is you that is on their mind.

Touches can be things like the flowers, coffee cups, an interesting article, postcards or a birthday card. They can be golf balls, calculators or shorts. They can be discount coupons, free tickets to an event, balloons or a gift card. It can be a phone call just checking in, a stopping by to say hello or an email making sure everything is okay. A touch is not necessarily a sales pitch but more of a reminder.

8.4. What to Gather During a Sales Call?

When I often teach new sales people about the sales call, they often get the impression that a sales call is to make a one call close. They feel that when you make a sales call that if you do not come away with a sale right on the spot that they have failed. I get this out of their mind right away because sometimes even in a quick close you need to gather some intelligence to make a great pitch.

When I owned my maintenance company and when I worked for the labor leasing company, I did something that I believe was very smart. Truthfully I had been doing it for years but as time moved on began to perform it seamlessly. I began to gather information every office I went to, every home I drove up to. What turned me on to this way of thinking is a book called Swimming with the Sharks by Harvey McKay.

The book is great but Harvey had created an idea that was called The Mckay 66. This was sixty six questions that Harvey had put together and what he had determined was that the closer that you would get to the answering of these 66 questions, the closer you were to a real relationship with your customers. After using this for years, I took it to a whole new level. Not only would I use the McKay 66 but I started to mentally take not of even more details when I would go and perform an estimate or talk to a prospect.

I have used it in many sales positions or company but I will focus on my maintenance company and I will walk you through what I set up mentally for myself and how I would use it. Most of the time when I would go to a house I would encounter a woman at the door 90% of the time. I throw this out there because it is important to understand. From the time I would pull up to the house I was already taking mental notes. You have to practice this unless you have a mind that will allow you to already do this. I had to train myself heavily in order to be successful. Upfront for you I would take notes as much as you can without getting found out.

When I would pull up to the house I was checking how well the landscape was kept up. I would look at and in the vehicles if I could. I looked for toys or garbage all over the front yard. I wanted to see if the paint was peeling or if the wood was rotten. I pushed the doorbell to see if it works and I would check the light fixture to see if it was falling down.

Once the person answered the door I would see if she was wearing a wedding ring. I would scan the room to see if it was clean and orderly or a chaotic mess. I scanned for family pictures on the wall. Then I would have them walk me around the house to look at what they needed repair taking very few notes. I would ask high gain questions here and there trying to get a feel for who I was dealing with.

You might be thinking that this sounds like a lot of work and tiring, but I became so efficient at it that it happened in minutes and I could obtain the information without much effort. If you can hone in this skill you will be very happy because once you gather enough information and understanding of who you are dealing with your sales will skyrocket!

Robert D. Kintigh

9. What do You Have in Common?

Previously I wrote about how we are strangers at first to our prospects when we first meet on a cold call and our mission is to become a warm lead as soon as possible. If we are going to become a warm lead then here is what I suggest you keep in mind; find commonality quickly. In the previous chapter I talked about gathering information on your prospects. We gather information to understand how to get them to buy and because we want them to get to know us. If you can find a common bond then making that personal connection is that much easier.

Most of the time, building that connection and bond that turns into a long term connection is easier in a commercial setting. It also works with residential customers but they are often not as easy to build a long term connection with. I did it for years but it is a skill in itself. No matter what I would try and make it happen especially if you are in a service business of any kind. Get those homeowners to like you and connect with you.

What do you have in common with your prospect? There are literally millions of things that you can have in common and that will catch the attention of your prospect or customer. My word of caution here is that you are sincere in everything you do. Do not fake liking something or having children because you will get found out. Always and I mean always be honest and sincere.

Things that you may have in common with someone is Nascar, children, married to a woman from a foreign country, baseball, football, a college you went to, coin collecting, golfing, reading, writing, boats, cars and on and on.

It is possible to not to be able to find something in common with someone as I have had it happen to me. You might think that it is harder to find things in common but I assure you that it is way easier than those people who you cannot find any commonality with. I absolutely can't believe it when I struggle to find something we both enjoy.

Another way to find something in common might be because of your parents or brother or in-laws. Use their love of something if you understand it. I would watch how you bring it up as it might just seem like a line but if you have enough material or mental facts then let it rip.

The reason finding something in common works is because it gives you a nice, easy way to open up the conversation. When two new people meet, this is often very tough to get going. If you have something you can talk about openly and excitedly, then you are well on your way to forming a relationship.

If you are not very interesting then you might need to take up some hobbies, watch some sports or read more books. People love it when they meet others who are in to what they are into. This is only going to happen if you have spent time learning new things, or engaging in something old you have been doing. To know baseball stats from 20 years ago may work with a few but current stats within the last 5 years means you are active in baseball. Go to work and find something in common.

9.1. How to Organize Your Calendar - Eliminate to do Lists

Have you ever noticed that the more you make to do lists that the more you feel stressed and pressured? Have you also noticed how the list only grows and never shrinks? This could be for many reasons and what is important is that we are making progress towards our goals. Let's take a look at how we can make sure we get done what we need to and not stress ourselves out in the process.

When you create a straight to-do list, you never have any priority to it except for two things. The first is to cross off as many as we can and two is that we often do the easiest stuff first so we can feel better about getting stuff crossed off. This may seem like a good idea but at the end of the day you are stressed and you may be no further along than when you started the day.

Every day we have things that we need to get done and the list always grows. We need to get done both personal and business activities and it always becomes a question what do I get done? Do you use a system to determine what you get done or do you do it like I described above? Let me first start by proposing an idea of what to do and when and then let's talk about how you can schedule your day and how to remove the stress. You can accomplish all that you desire if you go about it right!

To start with you should have on your schedule activities that are already on the books and you must leave room for things that come up that you can't necessarily schedule. For instance, if you need to pick up milk on the way home this is not easy to schedule ahead of time. You also don't want to be in schedule jail because you are so jam packed every day that there is no room for any flexibility. Again, this kind of planning causes stress and will not help you to feel charged during your day.

There are many systems out there that you might use but I am going to share one I learned years ago. Let me explain to you how I schedule my day and assign priority to my tasks that need to be done. Everything that I need to be done on a daily basis is scheduled in my planner. I used to use a Franklin Covey Planner and today I use my cell phone. What I do is assign a priority to my tasks. Everything is either an A, B, or C as well as a 1,2 or 3. An A is something that must get done! An A1 is top priority and an A3 is must get done but now first and as you go on down the line a B is something that is important but not a must or high priority and a C is something that needed but not a priority and can be moved till tomorrow or another day.

Why use these tags? Simple because it forces me to determine the importance of what I need to get done. It keeps stress off of me and all I have to work on making sure that gets done is the A's. Then if that occurs I can move on to the B's. Every once in a while I will do a C to get something easy done. This is as simple as I can help make it!

Something else I do ahead of time is I will fill up my schedule for two weeks. This is something to do either on day one of your new sales job or to stop and do it the first chance you get. You will never be effective trying to set your schedule the morning of every day. This is not a plan. This equates to making a to-do list and the equivalent to poor planning.

9.2. Why is Personal Growth Important?

No matter how smart that you may be or talented, personal growth is your key to more sales. The reason is that life, business and everything is always evolving and growing. In addition to needing to learn more about how people think, why you do the things you do and what it is going to take to become proficient as a top sales person. There is so much to learn and a life time is not even enough. You have to want to grow personally to even have a chance at your best.

In 22 plus years I have come across so many sales people who do not understand why they need to spend their free time with personal growth. It is as if they think that they should be paid to learn and grow. What I do not understand is why they don't learn on their own so they can get paid more. Doesn't that make more sense? Shouldn't you put into yourself so that you can maximize your worth and produce more income?

If you were to ask me where a good place to start is when it comes to learning more, I would probably say to start with working on observing more. I would send you to the mall and have you do some people watching where I would teach you to watch how people walk, how they talk, how they treat their kids, and how they act towards others. No words would need to be spoken just training your eyes and brain to see what is happening. Look at their body language and watch their movements. You will be surprised how quick you will learn some very interesting things about people.

Something else I would get you involved in is visualizing what you want. This is sort of a meditation time where you spend time with your thoughts and visualize what you really want in life. I took this a step further when I wrote a book called The Lies We Tell Ourselves where I laid out a 10 Essential Steps for Success where visualization is just one of the steps used to achieve or work through anything. I have lived by this for over 20 years and the process of visualizing is extremely powerful.

Most people struggle with the process of visualizing because if they can't see it they just can't believe it. This however is the main argument for visualizing. The whole point is that you need to see it first in order to make it happen and visualizing is the best way to make this clear in your mind. See it and believe it. Give it a try and you will be amazed at what you will learn and accomplish by doing this very powerful activity.

Personal growth is something you should start and never stop. It is a never ending process and the day you stop learning should be the day you should be dying. Until then you should get busy growing who you are and what you want to be.

I was introduced to books, books on tapes and seminars over 22 years ago and it has been one of the best things I could have done with the exception of learning to design my 10 step process. I accredit the majority of my sales to all of the personal growth that I have learned along the way. I am not telling you anything that I have not done so myself. I encourage you to find a program to get started with and then continue on the path to a better enlightenment of who you are.

9.3. Where to Find Prospects to Build Relationships

There are millions of places to find people and I will not bore you with all of the details. I will however give you some ideas of where to look and how to create a prospect list to work off of. I will get you started and then you will take it from there. I will just go down a list in no particular order.

Let's start with Google and depending on what kind of products or services you have this can be very strong for you. In some cases it may not help you but I will go through different ways to find prospects and how to utilize them. With the internet, networking and organizations, people are everywhere so we do not have a shortage of people. What you might really have is a shortage of relationships.

I use Google to research almost everything I need and the trick is not do you Google or not, but how you Google. You, me and everyone else thinks different and because of this reason we search different so try and search as many ways as you can to find what you are looking for. The greatest phonebook and research tool in the world is at your fingertips.

Networking groups are a strong way to meet people. Some groups you have to become a member and some you can just show up whenever the meetings are. There is a lot to be said about networking and is a book in itself but what I will tell you are that give more than you take and care about what you do. Help others get what they need and networking will work out well for you. You can Google to find these groups by the way. Search BNI, LeTips, FNI, local networking groups, business groups, chamber of commerce (your areas city) etc.

Facebook has over a billion people on it now and growing. If you have not figured out how to find people using this site then you should start. There is a search bar at the top similar to the way you might search on Google. Type in specific names, groups and industries and you will have results returned. Find people, start a conversation and build a relationship. Linkedin and twitter are two more powerful sites that you can locate people and build yourself a prospect list. The same concepts apply just like Facebook.

Your church is a great way to find prospects as these people would love to help you grow your business or occupation. Just because they go to your church doesn't mean they will automatically buy from you so treat them with the same respect as other prospects.

Ask people for referrals to people that they know especially if you have dealt with them in business and they seemed to enjoy working with you.   Referrals are powerful and are a great way to turn a cold call into a warm call.

Business or industry organizations which are often a membership type of group. Almost every industry has one or several so find out the ones in your industry.

I do not want to get too detailed because you should be able to get started with what I have provided but I am sure your biggest problem is not finding people but building relationships.

9.4. Does Relationship Building Work?

If you have read this far then I am hoping you are starting to understand that building relationships in sales is paramount to your success. If you are new to this concept or new to sales all together then you may not understand yet if relationship building works.

For some people this strategy is not quick enough and they want immediate gratification. Building relationships is a lot like the tortoise and the hair. It might seem a bit slow up front but the hair always wins the race.

Relationships are built in moments with people. They cannot be crammed or fast forwarded. They have to be carefully groomed and molded. Care needs to be taken and trust built in. There is no time limit on building a relationship and no real science. Some relationships happen quickly and get to a great place where others take long term work. There are many variables and there is no crystal ball to know how long they will take.

Here is why relationships work in sales; you have to do what I call drip marketing on your prospects and clients. What this means is that you are always just hanging about without annoying people but always dripping small and consistent messages so they remember you when it is time to buy. The stronger the relationship, the more they are likely to be accepting of you hanging out.

Tolerance will come from building these relationships and as a sales person this will be very helpful as we have a tendency to be one track minded at times. We so badly want to help and make a sale at the same time. Time is well spent when your prospects and customers really get to know you.

Relationships with people help because when others are interested in your success then your chances of success improve greatly. No one is an island unto himself. We need the help of others to achieve what we desire in business and in life. A relationship ensures that others are invested into your success.

The art of building relationships on a sales call comes down to thirty seconds; you get thirty seconds to make that eye to eye connection and draw them into you. If they perceive something that they do not like about you then you will struggle to ever gain any sense of relationship. People are *like driven* and if they like you then everything has a great chance of going well. If they do not like you, then you will struggle to make the connections that you desire.

Before I started using this sales technique, I thought all I ever had to do was create a great pitch and people will buy whatever I have to offer. You might be thinking this too and you will be partially right if you do because if you create a great pitch then you will generate some sales no doubt. There are definitely some great pitchmen and women in the world that make some great money. The average person however would not be considered a great pitchman or woman and this creates a problem.

The problem arises once the pitch has been delivered, then what? In a system where a pitchman/woman is used, the next person comes in and then the next person and everyone is part of a system to continue the sales process. If you are a one man/woman band then there is no one else to come in next for you so once the pitch is delivered the next process is to build the relationship. There is no better sales process in the world that leaves out this important element!

10. Why Will People Talk to You?

Have you ever asked yourself why would people talk to you? Think about it for just a moment; are you interesting? Do you create interest or draw intrigue? Why do prospects want to schedule a meeting with you or allow you to walk through the front door? Basically what I am asking is what makes you special?

If you have never owned a brick and mortar business, then you may not know that as a business owner with an office or building, people are always coming through the door with the next best thing. They come 5 days a week or however many days your doors are open. This kind of volume creates a problem for some but not everyone. What it creates is a lot of volume of what is called noise because it goes on continually. When they are not walking through the door, then they are calling on the phone, sending emails and texts.

If you learn to rise above this noise then you can become a very effective sales person. Most are too lazy or do not have a clue that they are ordinary and that they are not being seen because they are just like the last person who walked through the door or called on the phone. I do not mean to sound so negative, but the truth is they are too lazy to figure out what it will take to stand out, to make an impression and be seen. This takes work but the rewards are huge.

So how do we make a first impression? If you always use common sense and a bit of what I call *old school sales techniques*, then you will do just fine. Let's take a look at a few elements that will help set you a part from the rest.

The way you dress should reflect your level of success. Don't get caught up in if what you are wearing is appropriate for the industry. Get caught up dressing like someone who is successful. This is essential to projecting an image.

If you have a car that is a beater, make sure it is always spotless and do not park near the entrance. Project a successful image at all times and take no chances projecting a poor image.

Take care of your hands and don't let them feel like sand paper. You are a sales-professional and very few will be okay with shaking the hands of a person that is rough and not manicured. Cologne or perfume should be subtle and not over bearing. Make sure your socks match. Keep your shoes in good order. Dress for success.

Look people in the eye when you meet them and shake their hands. The hand shake is very important so do not be too aggressive and do not be too passive.

I still use words like "yes ma'am" and "no sir." I believe in showing as much respect as needed to prove that I am worthy of their attention. I tailor the language to my audience though as a word of caution as the younger generation will not appreciate it.

No matter what language you use, go as professional and respectful as possible. Give people a reason to want to talk to you. Make an impression and show your prospects that you are serious as a sales-professional.

This may be a dying art but I still think it works well and it should make a huge come back. I miss that old school way of doing business and the respect that used to be prevalent in the day to day dealings of business. I hope that we can make a difference and spread this mentality around. I promise it will make a huge difference to your business and bottom line. There are many who still enjoy this and more will if we spread it around enough.

10.1. Are You Building a Platform?

A platform is the stage that you get to stand on and talk to people from and the bigger the stage the more potential sales you will make. In today's world people meet you, hear what you have to say and then they tell you they will follow up with you. Once you leave or later on after the lunch they jump on Google and check out your company and you. Who is it that walked in the door, emailed them or called them is what they are searching to find out.

You may not sell on the internet but it does not matter anymore. People use search engines to check up on you and what you have told them. They want to see something that makes them feel better about you and they are hoping not to find negative information about you. They want to see that you are active and as successful as you are projecting. The facts are that today if you are successful in anything then it ends up on line.

Your platform will vary depending on the type of sales you are in and if you are online or offline. No matter how active you are on line, you should set up as much information as you can create about what you are doing. Check with your company and see what they will allow but no matter what you need to build your profile even if the company will not allow you to use their company info or logo.

You will want to tread lightly with your company and be respectful but your profession has to be about you. You may be with your current company for 20 years or just the next year but at the end of the day you need to build up who you are so that your platform carries on.

A platform and attraction marketing are very similar to one another. When you build out your platform, you are creating a resume or a show case of sorts for who you are. You do this to ultimately get people to buy from you and to be attracted to you. This will make the sales process so much easier. Think of it as creating P.R. for your brand. You are trying to extend your brand and get others to see the relevance of who you are.

There are many pieces that you want to set up and maintain and there are subjects that you want to cover. No matter what profession you are in, you want to build yourself a blog. Now maybe you have heard this before but let me try and give you reasons why you want to listen this time. A blog can set you a part in your industry.

You can write at least 3-4 times a week about something interesting about your industry, tips, ways to save money or find what someone really needs. You can teach people something new or tell stories. Every time you complete new blog you can email it to your prospects and customers. Show them you are a serious professional and are well informed. Plus while you are sending it to them, you will be creating your platform. Searches will be created by these new posts.

Next, make sure you are on twitter and Facebook. Post your new blogs there and let others see what you are all about. You might also post your blog to other places as well. There are plenty of places to get your blogged indexed. The whole point of what you are trying to accomplish is to get your voice heard. Let your potential prospects know about your expertise.

Blogging is only tough if you have nothing to say and we both know that is not you. You have many things to teach and give to people. You have put in the time and have an expertise.

10.2. Catching Their Attention

I have often prided myself on two aspects to which I am when it comes to making sales and building relationships; one is that I am able to speak well and intelligently and two I am self-educated on a lot of subjects. Am I bragging? No, not really but what it has done for me is open a lot of doors.

A lot of the people who you will come across in your sales career are bored and are looking to be intrigued. Not everyone but most are because most people would rather be doing something else. You can be that something else at least for the short period you are in front of them. You can be that reminder of an old childhood friend or you can remind them of someone they used to work with. You might remind them of a famous person or their next door neighbor.

You have many fine attributes and elements to who you are and you need to let them come out. You have people who will be attracted to who you are. They will like the way you talk, your ideas, your mindset, where you grew up and a number of other attributes that identifies who you are. Don't ever sell yourself short as there is so much to whom you are and others will find it interesting as long as you let it shine through!

One thing that helped me a long time ago become a great sales person is that I read a book called The Disney Way by Bill Capodagli and Lynn Jackson. There are many fine points in this book and it is very interesting but one of the things that really stuck in my head is about being on stage at all times. Disney employees have the mindset that they are always on stage and because of this they are always on their best. This includes their behavior, their performance and their actions. As a top sales person this should resonate with you in a way that starts to mold and form your mind into the best sales person ever! Act as if you are on stage and never give a bad performance.

When you communicate with prospects and customers, make sure that you are always using positive words and optimistic outlooks. Watch joking with them in inappropriate ways. Use common sense in how you speak to them and do not allow yourself to get too comfortable. Always stay on the respectful side of things as you will never go wrong with this attitude.

I have spent the better part of twenty years making sure that I am memorable in everything I do. I do not look to do things as others do as I am constantly making sure I stand out on my own. There is plenty of average in this world and I do not be one more of them knocking on your door. You might be thinking what can I do when I sale cleaning products? How can I be different? I would say to that I took an industry called construction and I made it shine. I turned on my showmanship and made every sales call in a clean vehicle, hair was always neat, clothes were right and tight and my language and body language was professional.

If I can get noticed in the construction industry and make a huge impression so can you no matter what your industry is. Don't make excuses. What I urge you to do instead is create raving fans of your craft and have them telling everyone they know.

10.3. Mental Aspects to a Daily Grind

When something is new we tend to get very excited. When we start out in sales the same will hold true. You took the position because you liked what you heard and saw in the product or service. You saw the opportunity behind it and then you got very eager to get going so you can set the world on fire.

Day one arrives and you are nervous but extremely excited. You dig in and you go to work. When you first get going, things get a little tough and you discover that there is a lot of work upfront as you learn your products or services. Then that magic happens that we all look forward to; a sale happens. You are pumped and even more excited. Day 30 and you are making sales and things are moving along but the excitement has leveled out. Day 60 and now you are feeling burned out a bit and need to rejuvenate yourself. What has happened?

Look, don't panic just yet as we all go through it in sales and in business. Some take longer for it to happen and others go through it quicker but either way it happens to us all. What you need to learn is how to manage what will happen.

The mental aspect comes into play in every part of sales. The psychology behind what we do is so important but nothing may be more important than the mental aspect of our mindset. You are in a profession that will have ups and downs, rejection, is often grueling and people will at times be ignorant to what you have to offer. You will put up with a lot during your sales career. Not to mention the repetition of your days, the meetings, the phone calls and more. Your mindset is going to be your best tool provided that you maintenance it on a regular basis.

When you begin to feel yourself getting a little burned out, I make sure that I change things up and I throttle things down. You may think that you can handle it or keep on pushing on but you will find out that you are wrong. We all have different thresholds but at some point collapse will occur if you don't rejuvenate. Do not be ashamed or feel like you are not a champion. Champions in sports, business or anything else will always make sure that they rest the mind and their body. When all is 100% then they push hard.

Once when I worked for this company in Seattle, the owner had flown in to check on us and he learned I was taking 10 days off to go out of town and he almost chastised me for wanting to do this. I worked almost 7 days a week for 10 months and I could feel that I was burned out. He should have given me a bonus to enjoy myself but instead tried to make me feel bad. I had no remorse because when I came back I was on fire! The time did me so much good. I read two books and created a ton of ideas to implement all the while having fun and relaxing.

Some days will be so easy to spring out of bed and some days will be tough. That is just the way the game is played. My baseball coach had it right when he said to always operate on one level. Never get too high and never get too low. Conserve your energy for the long haul and never give up. These are great words for any sales professional.

10.4. Who Do You Mirror?

When you want to be a top salesperson does it not make sense to find someone who has already been there? A mentor to talk to, listen to or learn from is priceless. This could be someone famous or this could be the top dog in your company and nothing would be better than mirroring what they are doing.

When you mirror with someone who has it figured out, you are seeing it live what needs to be done. Body language, words and eye contact are observed at first hand. Take notes and pick their brains as much as you can.

In my younger days, I had the luxury and pleasure to work with some very good people. I learned early on to not act like a know it all or even as if I had more figured than I really did. People will help you out so much more when you are open minded and not a know it all. You have to be humble and open your ears and shut your mouth. That is tough for me but I have mastered it my whole life so I know you can too!

If there is no one to learn from where you work or the opportunity you are involved with or you have little to no respect for those around you then seek someone out. You will be surprised that there are a ton of people out there that would be glad to mentor you. You can also seek out someone commercially as with today's technology you can learn as you go or on demand.

What you are looking for is to learn from someone who has been successful in the past and present if still active. You need to learn what their magic is and if it is a fit for you. There are book smarts and then there is real world knowledge and that is what you are seeking. You can learn the book stuff but you want secrets and experience knowledge. The good ones will always share with you as to be a top producer is usually a giver and will give what they know. Some will not and so you will just have to keep on searching.

The things you want to focus on when looking for a mentor or coach is someone who has a proven track record. You need someone you can respect and understand. You need someone who lives a life that you admire. You want a people's person who people seem to like and respect and love dealing with. You do not want mediocre or ordinary in the mentor that you are seeking.

If you have never had a mentor before I would urge you to get one. You will benefit a lot from doing this and can take your career to an entire new level. The insights can be so valuable and the mental training will be to your advantage.

If having a mentor is so powerful then why do more sales people not get one? I believe it is because they are afraid as to what it might mean to their status. They get worried others might think that they are not very good at their job. The truth is that you will be seen as smarter, more successful and someone who seeks advice when they need to learn more. Find a mentor and ask to mirror them and learn from them.

Robert D. Kintigh

11. Learn to Break Some of the Rules

I say this with the most care because what I really mean is to break, ignore, bend and twist a lot of the rules but I do not want you to get fired or in trouble. Breaking the rules is not about violating important policies and procedures. What it is about is learning what it will take to break out from the crowd. Rules are for protecting the face of the company and for keeping some sense of control with the bulk of the employees. They are guidelines for people to follow and structure that some people need. You are not a part of those people who need structure or guidelines. You are creative and are ambitious and you are looking to do extraordinary things and that might require you to tweak some rules.

The main idea is not to break the rules for the sake of breaking the rules. In fact it is not even about thinking about the rules but more about what it is going to take to be a top sales person. You are going to have to figure out your strategy as you go because you really have three things to always consider:

1. Do you do something that maybe is a bending of the rules and ask for forgiveness later?
2. Do you ask for permission to break the rules?
3. Do you do what you need and there is no violation to worry about?

Again, you will think first and then decide if there is an issue with what you want to do in your sales position. This may or may not give you comfort but I do not know of any top sales person who never broke the rules. They all have a common bond and that is that they do things different than everyone else. In fact I can make an argument that you are well on your way as a top sales person when this comes more into play for you.

The way I describe all of this breaking of the rules I attribute to a leadership mentality. When you are willing to step out more and lead the way then you will have to deal more with this. As a leader who is aspiring to be a top sales person, it is very difficult to obey all of the rules. You will not have the intention to break rules but it will get in your blood. You will have a need continually to reach further and stretch harder to greatness.

Your company has a dilemma. They need to keep order and preserve integrity all the while they need leaders like you to break out and be a superstar. This is nerve racking for whoever is in charge because they are always saying get out of the box while they are always stuffing people back in the box. They mean well but they have not figured out what to do about this situation.

What I would suggest is that you study the policies and procedures especially the ones that will get you immediately terminated. Of course if you break any laws then all bets will be off and you will be fired but most rules you break will probably be minor so life and death is not an issue but don't do anything unprofessional and you will be okay. I used to fax way more than one of the companies I worked for liked but it worked very well for me and because of that I was given forgiveness and cover by my general manager. You can find the same respect when you break out!

11.1. Simple Sales Tips 101 to Live by and Remember

#1 - Remember you are always there to help people and not just sell something.
#2 - Always be patient and do not over pressure people.
#3 – People love to buy and hate to be sold.
#4 – What separates what you have from the competition is you so work on being your best.
#5 - Persistence is the key to winning.
#6 – Never be lazy about anything that you do.
#7 – Smile often and be easy to talk to.

#8 – Educate and inform people and do not just regurgitate information about your product or services.

#9 – People buy from those people they know, like and trust so you have to let them get to know you.

#10 – Ask questions and get answers to how to create sales.

#11 – Pay attention and find additional sales.

#12 – If your paycheck is too small then all you have to do is work harder and smarter.

#13 – People are everywhere but relationships need to be found.

#14 – To make a million dollars in sales, you need to think like a million dollar producer.

#15 – If you want to be number one, then work harder than anyone else and think harder than anyone else!

#16 – Luck is not mystical. It is made by top producers by their actions which really makes it intentional. Turn over more rocks than anyone else and find what you need and want!

#17 - Turn over more rocks than anyone else and find what you need and want!

#18 – When you are feeling burned out, take time off and relax and refresh your mind.

#19 – Don't let others stop you in your tracks. Be the force to be reckoned with.

#20 – The top producer in your company or field was once on the bottom.

#21 – I am the top producer because that is my mindset!

#22 – Don't position yourself like the plague and people will not run from you.

11.2. Time to Get Moving to the Top

I have given you everything that you need to start on the road to being a top sales person. I have given you 22 years of sales knowledge. Everything that I have written here has worked for me and it can work for you. You want to build a sales profession up that will feed you for years to come and my methods will help you do that as long as you will be open to giving it a try. You deserve to be a top sales person and being the best is easier than you think.

What will separate you from the pack? Do things others are not willing to do. Go farther than anyone else. Work harder and longer. Be more determined and never give up. You will find if you observe others who are in the profession that they will not push very hard. They talk a good game but ultimately that is what it is; just talk.

You can build residual income by building relationships. If you build a solid foundation with people then they will come back to buy over and over again. This is a strong way to build your wealth. People will buy from you when they like you or perceive a value far bigger than what they pay and a strong relationship will cement that.

Where will you start to build your territory? How will you set yourself up to be the best? It all starts with you and your mindset. You know many years ago I was just not sure if I could be the best and I had no idea how to really connect with people. I worked hard and I tried learning all that I could. I spent most of my time trying to sell and treated people like numbers. I would just move on to the next when it didn't work in my favor. I started having more success when I stopped this madness. Build relationships and never stop learning.

You will have all the success you desire if you will give it your best and desire to be the best. I wish you the greatest time ever as the top sales person and wish you all that you desire.

12. Networking Introduction

Word of mouth advertising for business has greatly changed these days and waiting around for people to be referred to you and your company takes too long for most people. Word of mouth is powerful for a business. Word of mouth is when one person engages services or products with a company and they have a great experience and then they tell others about that company. Then when that person needs your products or services they call on you based upon the recommendation of the person who has used your services or products already. The good part is that they feel like they know you and trust you based upon the referral. The bad part is that if you want to bring on a hundred new jobs or orders, you will need to do work for others that will refer you to others over a period of time. This technique for building your business can take some time.

There is no doubt that word of mouth advertising is powerful and your business can benefit greatly from this concept, but the time factor often takes years to really pay off. What is an alternative that is quality like word of mouth, but pours rocket fuel on the idea? The simple answer is networking with other people looking for word of mouth advertising just like you.

If networking is so powerful then why isn't everyone doing it? Some do not know about it, some go about it wrong and some are doing it as I write this book. If you are just now discovering networking then my hopes are that you will benefit from all of the hard work that others have done in order for you to discover it. Networking is brilliant in so many ways and when you participate the right way, you will begin to see the power of word of mouth advertising with rocket fuel.

I have benefited from being a part of many networking groups along the way. I have been a part of BNI which is Business Networking International, FNI which is Free Networking International, meetup.com, church groups, chambers of commerce, LeTip and many other groups of this nature.

What networking group is the right group for you? That is a difficult question for me to answer for you. I am going to introduce you ways to discover the right group for you, elements of a good group and how to interview the members of the group.

As an organization or company, you will use or be a part of networking as a primary tool to help facilitate sales for your products, services or any other type of sale. We use other marketing techniques as well to grow our business, but networking should be 80% of your business model.

In any given city, there are thousands and thousands of small businesses, yet probably only about 20% go to networking groups, this still equates to approximately 20,000 small businesses in your local area in networking. It will take a long time to just get through these 20,000 people. Networking is a phenomenal way to get in front of willing participants who need your services and will gladly schedule a one-on-one coffee appointment with you.

Businesses that attend Networking Groups:
- Buy from those they know, like and trust
- Give testimonials about others in their group
- Are willing participants
- Understand one-on-one appointments and setting them
- Are great advertisers/marketers for you
- Are serious about growing their businesses

We use Networking because it works, PERIOD!

If you have never spoken in front of a group, do not panic as generally 99% of networking groups will be very welcoming and treat you very well. If you fear public speaking then networking will help you get over it as it is a regular routine at meetings. Do not shy away from it because of your fear. I would encourage you to face it.

All networking groups are always looking for new members to increase their effectiveness. They need visitors, new members and great power partners. They need you too as much as you need them. Networking is only as effective as you make it. We will cover the process later but networking is a complete system. If you chose to only use a portion of the system then you will only make a portion of the sales. Use the whole system on a daily basis, us the whole system, enjoy all of the profits.

Networking can be free but some organizations do charge a membership fee and a breakfast fee. We cover all fees associated with networking that are mandatory. Utilize what these networking groups offer to the fullest.

Why do you want to be a member of a Networking Group?

For the long run, these groups will become a very effective breeding ground for people and businesses to sign up with you. They will not only sign up with you but they will also send multiple referrals on a regular basis to you. They will essentially become your marketing department. Let me introduce you to the idea of coffee meetings or one to ones and why you want to incorporate them into your networking.

Why do we set up coffee appointments or one-on-one appointments when we are a part of networking?

We set up coffee appointments because it is your best vehicle to learning more about how you can help your prospect/member to grow their business. You need to understand them face to face and show them that you genuinely care about helping them grow their business. When you set the appointment, allow no more than 45 minutes. Do not talk for the first 30 minutes.

I can't stress this enough. If the client sits down and immediately says "tell me about how this works or about what you do" or something of that nature, you must resist the urge to tell them everything not start in. Say to them, "First, do you mind telling me about your business? You sound like you have the coolest job in the world" Spin the focus back on them and do not be eager to be all about you. This is the 30/15 rule. Thirty minutes for them and their business and fifteen minutes for you to talk about you and your business. Give it a try and you will be amazed how well that it works.

When it is your turn to speak, keep it short, simple, and basic. Your job is to give them a 15 minute overview of something interesting about who you are and what you do. Your job is simple; let them get tell about who they are and give them a reason to want to know more about you.

Where you decide to set your coffee appointments is determined by location of the networking group and to find a quality facility that is professional. You should determine your location ahead of time, previous to your network meeting. Have a coffee location set ahead of time and the times you have allotted before you go to the networking meeting. Be prepared ahead of time and have times available to ask people to join you and you will get way more yes's than if you have to call them later to schedule.

Places that I like to use are clean, professional, well known and comfortable. Some of the places I have used in the past are coffee places like Starbucks, eating places like Panera Bread, Chilis, TFI Fridays or a local place or country clubs, or meeting spaces. I am not a fan for meetings at McDonald's, Dunkin Donuts or loud and uncomfortable locations as well as fast food places. You need a place you are not shouting at and that you can make a connection with people one to one.

Taking notes is a must and never be afraid to do so. It shows you are a professional, are serious about what you are doing and genuinely care about the person you are meeting with. If you are going to take the time to meet with someone in person you might as well get all that you can from it.

The other networking I want to introduce you to is networking on line. Some people think that you can't build a quality relationship on line and pass business around the internet. I will show you how to make it possible and deliver quality to the referral game.

Networking is the same on line as it is in person when it comes to going about building business relationships. You still need to be honest in your efforts, learn to listen and figure out a way to help people. I will show you how to accomplish this and take your business to a whole new level.

I am not saying that networking is everything to your business. What I am saying is that it is a must for your business and no matter how you go about participating in it, you should make sure that your business gets every chance possible to be discovered and to allow others to help you grow it. Like all of my other books I will provide a simple, straight forward look at the practice of networking and will provide you with resources and ideas to make your business the best that it can be.

The last part of this introduction on Networking is that as an entrepreneur it is often lonely and can stunt your ideas and your social skills. Networking can help you with creativity and your relationship building.

12.1. What is the Act of Networking

The act of networking is taking what you know and who you know and sharing them with others to help them grow their businesses. Networking is a group of people who work together to help each other out in business. It is a sharing of networks with each other without the worry of losing anything for your business. Networking is an accountability system where everyone works together to ensure the integrity of the group. Networking is a system of passing referrals and supporting fellow business owners. In short, the act of networking is a business building tool for business owners everywhere.

How do you share what you know and who you know to help others? First of all, just because you joined the group it doesn't mean everyone in the group is suddenly trustworthy. That is why step one is really to get to know as many as you can right away so expect to be busy upfront. You can accomplish this by phone, email, coffee meetings, education classes or meetings. You joined for a reason so you must be prepared to engage this way as anything less will not help you very much. You must get to know the people in your group so you can decide who you will open up your contacts to or what you know.

Who you know is your list or contact sphere. They are people that you have some kind of relationship with. These people need to be protected until you know you can share them with others. Do not rush it and feel pressured to open up and share people right away. Start slow with contacts who are consequential and not a business killer. Casual connections area a great way to start and then as you build trust with your members, you can open up more and more as you see fit. The act of networking is about building relationships and trust.

The act of networking is about extending your network, helping others extend theirs and learning how to make it happen by helping other people first. The act of giving is a very powerful tool but is often difficult for some to figure out how to perform helping others first. I assure you that although not easy at first, it becomes easier the more you work with the idea.

The techniques I discuss about networking can be used in person or on line. Concepts like helping others first can be performed in so many ways and I want to show you the possibilities of using this mindset. Once you put it to work you will begin to see a whole new action and reaction to you and your brand.

Most business owners and middle managers and entrepreneurs often get focused on one thing; how can I get people to buy from me? I get it and it makes sense to some degree but let's look at some very important understandings about this thinking that is not really doing a lot for your company. When I say learn how to help others first, I am talking about putting other people's needs first before yours. You might have just found that hard to hear but I promise you will get it. Let's take a look at some interesting facts and ideas and see if I can convince you to change your mind set about marketing.

If you shout out to the world about your company you will likely grab some people's attention. If you can get others to shout out about your company then you will get much more attention. Think about that for a moment. Is this not one of the most powerful reasons that social media is so powerful? When someone else talks about you or your service, their friends and other people tend to take notice because they believe it must be sincere and honest. This is a powerful element of networking both on line and off line.

What about you? Don't you feel better about a product or service once you hear it from someone else? Doesn't it make you feel safer about spending your money knowing someone else stands behind what you do or have for sale. I am sure the answer is yes it makes you feel better so that is why networking is powerful.

Maybe I am starting to convince you about networking groups, but you are still skeptical it is effectiveness on line. I am sure that if I gave you just want one example where this idea or method is powerful online then you will totally understand its power. I will provide you with one powerful example for now in the hopes that it will lend more strength to my argument why you want to network both on and off line.

Have you ever heard of a website called Amazon? You probably know about Amazon but what you may not know is that the retail giant made its mark on the world by doing one powerful thing; they implemented a review and rating system on all of their products and vendors. This is the same as the power of the testimonial in your local BNI or Chamber of Commerce or any other networking group.

Amazon had it figured out early when they implemented this system of testimonies because it has literally been single handed for making everything else that Amazon is about a huge success. You might try and argue it is because of pricing or comparison on the site but that element of being able to decide if you trust something through the experiences of others is extremely powerful and if it works for Amazon then it can work for you.

As we continue on in this book we will discuss the different ways to get involved with networking, some of the techniques I have used and ways to maximize everything that you need to do with networking. What is important to understand is that there is this tool that will open many doors for you and your business.

The act of networking begins with you and the understanding of how to be a great networker. The next thing important to learn is about finding the right group or groups. What is the right group for you? First, you need to understand that there are generally a couple of types of groups.

One type of group will only allow you in one group similar to theirs which is groups that allow only one business per industry. For instance, BNI will only allow you in BNI if you are in another group as a carpet cleaner and hold that seat exclusively.

When you join BNI you agree to not engage in another group exclusively for your industry as they allow you to take the seat for the group as a carpet cleaner or whatever business you are in. You can join the chamber as they do not hold one type of seat per industry.

I am sure you will discover your type of networking group as we continue on with our journey of discovering networking. There are free groups, memberships, chambers and industry specific groups.

12.2. Learning About Networking Groups

Let's first start with BNI as an organization and discuss how the group operates and what is expected of you as a member of the organization. The first thing to know is that the organization is run by Dr. Ivan Misner and BNI is set up like a Franchise. Every area is run and managed by an owner. They belong to the system and are supported by BNI as a corporate entity. BNI is a well oil machined and has a very aggressive plan in place to continue expansion and dominate as the biggest and best networking organization.

The organization allows business owners to visit each BNI twice before they have to join. That means that you can visit every BNI in the area or around the country for that fact before you must join one. If you do not join one after two visits you are not allowed back. The meetings are generally Monday through Thursday from 7:30 a.m. until 9:00 a.m. You generally arrive at least 15 minutes before so you can mingle.

As a rule of thumb, every BNI member needs to bring a guest at least once a month. There are exceptions to the time and day as each chapter can decide the time and day they wish to meet but the idea is to be as uniform as possible no matter which chapter you go to.

The meeting which is run on point for an hour and a half is a commercial for an hour and a half about BNI. I don't say this to make any point except to inform you how the whole thing is operated so you can decide if it is for you or not. Do not also expect much variance to the meeting as what you see as a visitor you will see as a member. This is done purposefully and is meant to create a sense of familiarity and predictability.

When you join the BNI you are not allowed to miss when you feel like it. As previously discussed you are allowed to miss 3 times in a 6 month period and 3 more if you have a sub. If you miss more than the allotted time given then you will be banned from BNI forever. Seems harsh maybe but they are looking for serious and responsible business owners who are going to take responsibility to the group seriously. If you are going to consider joining BNI then I urge you to learn all of the rules upfront. BNI is serious about the rules and some might even say they are militant about their rules.

You might want to join BNI because you like structure or you want to make sure that your time is spent right. The one thing I can guarantee is that the members show up to BNI meetings. This makes your time very effective and well spent.

There are a number of chamber groups in any given area. If you live in Seattle for instance you could Google Seattle Chamber of Commerce or whatever city you live in and find the chamber near you. The good thing about the Chambers are that they are open to new members as long as you pay your membership fees which are usually three hundred to five hundred dollars a year. They usually have micro groups as well that are seat specific but the chamber as a whole is open to all industries.

There is usually one main lunch or meeting a month with one weekly meeting in the morning. Of course it varies by chamber but this gives you a general idea. What I like about the chambers is the wide diversity of people who come into a chamber of commerce. It gives you a wide variety of people to meet, build relationships with and to extend your brand with.

What I am not too fond of is that often times the Chamber attracts people who just like to belong to a group and love going to coffee meetings on a regular basis. They just do not seem at times to be committed to building their businesses. I have a few times been chastised about getting down to business in a chamber meeting which blows my mind away. This is not everyone who joins a chamber of course but this group is definitely different from a BNI or a LeTip group. Overall the chamber is a great way to meet people and extend your brand but you will have to figure out the flavor of the group you join and operate accordingly.

There are a number of other groups out there I have been a part of like Free Networking International and Le Tip as well as Meetup.com and trade organizations. The best thing to do is to Google them and type in things like networking groups, business networking, chamber of commerce, builders associations, etc.

Whatever industry you are in there is a group or groups for you as well as generally networking groups. You must try out several before you plant yourself in one of them.

What you need to understand overall is that when you join or visit a networking group you will be taken back a bit to high school as even as adults we get into clicks and limited mindsets. I do not say this to be offensive. I just want to point out that if you are not used to networking then you may get a little uncomfortable at first because of the nature of groups of people. They will have their clicks and same people they sit and hangout with. Be bold and break into the group and be outgoing and allow people to get to know you. Do not shy off or hide out or become intimidated.

Also, no matter how good or bad a group may be make sure that you stick to one very important element of what you are trying to do and that is to stay in the business of building your business and not running the group. Running the group should always be secondary if it fits with your overall plan for your business. If it does not fit then

you cannot get wrapped up into it.

In a short while I will give you one of my systems I used as a visitor which I have never done openly except to those who I have hired to work for me. Once you read that section you will better understand what I am about to tell you about each group you visit. I feel that I need to tell you about this here as learning about groups brings up a talent you should develop if you are going to be great at networking.

What I became really great at is showing up to a group and getting a real good feel on what I like to call the flavor of the group. The term may seem a little weird but the idea is that every group has a theme or taste or flavor to who they are as a group. This is important to learn quickly so that you can decide if the group is right for you or not. Let me explain further about the flavor.

The flavor of a group is first off how they act the minute you walk in the door. Some groups are overly excited when visitors arrive while others act as if they could care less. Some groups are even keeled and others are suspicious. Some groups have a high participation rate while others host a timid fanfare. There is a group for everyone and it is your job to figure out the group that fits who you are, what you want to become and that will help generate the most business for your business.

12.3. Learn the System of Helping

I have said it over and over again when I write about business matters and building a business; learn to help others first and then your needs will be better served in the long run. This will never work for selfish people and those who don't understand how to use their business to help others. My hope is that I can at least help the ones who do not understand. Selfish people can only fix themselves and until that happens; you will never understand where I am coming from.

No matter how great a business or an entrepreneur is put together they all need help. They need help marketing their business, finding new prospects, gathering more resources, looking for employees, training, and employee education and on and on. Every business needs help of some sort and you can position yourself as the helping entrepreneur.

You want to build a reputation as a member who helps others first. Talk about a way to go viral, try helping others and see how fast the message spreads. You will be known as the go to person and others will be willing to tell others about you and your business without hesitation. You can spend all kinds of money on advertising or marketing and you may never get the return you do with helping others first.

Telling you to help others first is easy to say and a little harder to figure out at first. You will need to train yourself on the technique but after a while it becomes second nature. You literally have to train yourself to look for opportunities for others. You have to keep your ears open at all times to understand what your fellow networkers need. In short, learning to help others is a skill that you must work on especially if you have been solely focused on helping your own business first.

My favorite way to help others is to look for their pains and then figure out how to help them. If you find I have a pain and you figure out how to heal me then I am forever grateful. If I have a want and you help me then I will be grateful and will try and help you back.

That is the real secret isn't it? As human beings we can't help but to help those who help us. It is like giving a gift as the receivers will more than likely becoming a giver. Not all will reciprocate as again some people are selfish and are takers but most will want to give back. Do not focus on the takers. Do your part and if all they do is take, then you will and should move on.

The idea of gift giving goes back since the beginning of civilization so

it should be no surprise to you that I say to help others first. We can do so much good by focusing on others and helping them spread the message about their business. It is just an entirely new way to look at things that should take you in a direction that allows you to relax and be generous. It should not tire you or frustrate you as you are not uptight about you and your business. You should be care free and not be so concerned about the bottom line but the relationship bottom line.

When you help others just do it and then do not bring it up. You help others in the hope that it speaks for itself and should never need to be bragged about. What you do for others is the calling card and no commercial is needed. If there is no recognition then move on and help again. I promise you that eventually it will be noted if you are a champion of helping.

Robert D. Kintigh

13. My BNI System of Networking

BNI stands for "Business Networking International". The BNI organization is built around the theme of "a givers gain" or "givers get". What this means is that they teach their members to give first in order to get value or help in return! They are taught many ideas and below is a list of things to understand:

- They are taught to have coffee appointment/one-on-one's
- They must bring visitors monthly
- They are taught to become your marketing department
- They buy first from members then from members referrals
- They will buy from you because they want you to join their BNI
- They must be at their meeting and cannot miss more than Six times in a Six Month period. Three absents and three substitutes and no more.
- They stand up every meeting and profess business they have for others, closed business from other members and CEU's (Continuing Education Units) completed.
- BNI is really structured and has many processes and structures in place as an organization. What we do is engage in BNI's based upon their mode of operation.

We want to make it clear that BNI is an immediate component of your organization and you must engage and go to BNI's immediately to see why we say this. The BNI's are your fast track for getting immediate exposure provided you follow the 8 steps below

This is an example we used for our business but you can adapt it to help you in the same way.
8 Step Program

Step 1: It is imperative that <u>each</u> of the three salespeople go to a Tuesday, Wednesday, and Thursday BNI. (If they can go to a 4th

BNI on Friday, that's a bonus.)

Step 2: They will find that the average BNI meeting has 25 attendees. BNI passes around a box with every business card. Each salesperson needs to pick up every card.

Step 3: The salesperson will need to say the 30 second commercial during the meeting.

Step 4: After the BNI meeting, our salesperson should be the **LAST** to leave. After the meeting, they need to seek out and ask qualified BNI members if they could meet us for a "One-on-One" meeting for us to learn about their business, for us to learn what a good lead is for them, and for us to review our workshop. Note: We ask them to meet for a One-on-One, not to sell them our workshop, but to learn about their business and what a good lead is for them.

Step 5: Go to Starbucks or Panera Bread (location of One-on-One meetings) and sort BNI business cards into A, B, C & D piles. Of the 25 attendees 40% or about 10 will be A or B qualified.
      A = spoke to person at BNI meeting, they agreed to a One-on-One. (May need to call them for exact day and time)
      B = in a good industry, but has not agreed to meet One-on-One yet
      C= in an ok industry, but has not agreed to meet One-on-One (example ok industries are Commercial real estate, doctors, dentists)
      D = not an appropriate industry for federal government contracting (examples of inappropriate industries are, fund raiser, financial advisor, public adjuster, merchant credit card, professional organizer, MLMs like Prepaid legal, Shaklee, Amway, etc., mortgage brokers, Feng Shui consultant, residential realtors, dry cleaners, sports marketing, bankers, lawyers such as real estate, criminal, personal injury, estate, & family)

Step 6: Call immediately that morning for 45 minute One-on-One coffee meetings with all A and B leads. **The goal is 18 One-on-Ones meetings this week!** You should be able to make appointments with 60% of the A / B leads.

Step 7: Conduct the 45 minute One-on-One meeting following the 30 - 15 rule. The **30 - 15 rule** says, you make them talk about their business and what's a good lead for them for the FIRST 30 minutes, then you talk for last 15 minutes. You must open your 15 minute conversation with the story of how your company was founded. We use to make sure we placed a special emphasis on how the government consultant business model (Free 2 hour Seminar followed by $4,000 - $5,000 2 1/2 day seminar where they only get 80-90% of what they need, followed by $10k -$20k monthly consultant fee) is compared to our 1/2 day, $497 workshop where they get 100% and no hidden agenda for consultant fees. If this is presented up front, you'll rarely have push-back on the $500 workshop fee.

Step 8: Ask them to attend the workshop. Each salesperson will close 1 out of 4 One-on-One meetings. Therefore, with 18 One-on-Ones, they close between 4 - 6 workshop participants.

Step 8.5 For some you'll need to call them the next day to give them a day to think about it.

The BNI's generally meet Monday through Thursday and sometimes on Fridays. Once you become a member of a BNI, you will continue to schedule one-on-one's (coffee appointments) and do your part to contribute to the group so you will reap the rewards of membership. If you only take, you will not receive. You must be genuine in trying to help your fellow members. Please take a word of caution however and do not get involved with running the BNI, you are in the coaching business and not the BNI business.

BNI's are generally free to guests but on occasion you may get charged. The above example is what we used to supply our Federal Government Specialists who would sell workshops to BNI members. I show you this because I want to make it clear how serious we were about our business as how far we would go to do everything to the fullest.

I have shown this to others but what I am about to tell you now has never been made public before as it has been a well-kept secret to a lot of success of mine and others who have worked for me in the past. I also am not out to make BNI look bad in any way. I believe they are a quality organization and they deserve a lot of respect. What I simply did was this; I played the game and knew the rules. Here is my BNI system to making a lot of money.

The above training is given first so that our people could understand this next step. Here is what I taught them after doing extensive research:

Since BNI is built on the concept of givers gain, we would leverage this to get coffee appointments and other help. We would first map out all of the BNIs in the area with times and day mapped out as well as the name of the BNI, the location they would meet and the president and area directors as well as the franchise owner. We would then take a put it all on a spread sheet and then add in where all of the local Panera's and Starbucks were as well as some alternatives for meeting people.

We then would plan it all out for the next 60 days. Which meetings the specialists would go to go to and when, where the coffee meetings were held with time slots set up for both the meeting and the coffee appointments. Once all of this was set up for each specialist we would then go into the next phase of training. I would call it the approach and landing method.

The meetings generally started at 7:30 a.m. and the specialist was instructed to be at the BNI location at about 7:00 a.m. no later. They were to park somewhere diagonal from the front door but not on top of the front door if it was possible. I will tell you the reason in a minute but keep in mind that no detail is trivial and is very important.

The next step in the process was to gather your belongings and get out of your car. Do not go anywhere just yet until you see someone pull up that you know is a BNI member and that you think will be a great meeting partner. Chemistry is very important and for this exercise it is no different. You will know they are there for the meeting and a part of the BNI because they will generally have some sign on their car and will look the part.

As they start to get out of their car start walking towards the front door slowly looking a little lost. Do not look hopeless and unprofessional but having a look of confusion on your face is important. Now is about the time why I tell you why not to part to close to the door as well as do not walk to quickly to the front door especially if more than one pulls up. I also want to remind you of another BNI rule and that is that members must bring at least one visitor a month.

So as I walk timidly to the front door, looking a bit lost I look over at the BNI member and ask, "is this where the BNI meets?" The member will answer generally very eagerly and say, yes!" You then ask them if they would mind if you were their guest for the meeting. If they are not brain dead they will say yes or of course.

You still want to be far enough away from the door that you can make a proper introduction and get to know this person as much as possible. Do not go through the door with just a name. I also want to point out that you have just given them a huge gift as most struggle with bringing a guest once a month. Givers gain is already in play here and you are ahead of the game. Who do you think owes you a coffee appointment first?

Now that you know something about your host, walk through the front door with them as if you are old friends and do not let on you just met in the parking lot. Your host will probably get you signed in, pay for your breakfast and get you a seat and come back for you and direct you to the breakfast spread. Next they will walk you around and start to introduce you to the others in the group. Collect business cards along the way and if you do not get them all do not worry as they will pass around a business card box during the meeting.

The meeting will start right at 7:30 a.m. (if that is when the meeting is scheduled for) and is as automatic as a church bell ringing at 12:00 noon. The meeting will run for an hour and a half on the time, all the time. During the meeting they will profess business passed on to other members and the yearly total of referrals past to all members. They give testimonials about fellow members and while this is going on a business card box is passed around. Usually two members each week will give what is called their ten minute, which is a ten minute presentation of what they are about. Reports will be given about the chapter and the meeting will end.

At the beginning of the meeting and at the end you have a very important task and that is to fill up your coffee appointment calendar while you are fresh in their minds starting with the one you gave the gist to in the first place. Present to them two times either that day or the next.

Those who are serious will schedule with you and those who are not will tell you to call them. Those who make appointments with you are checked off the list and those who do not need to be followed up until they meet with you or until they tell you to get lost and then you still follow up with them one more time. BNI is a structured system you can benefit from and the members can too!

13.1. Online Networking for Beginners

If you have never networked on line or are struggling to understand how to network on line, then I hope that I can shed some light on the subject and I can help you to improve this very important skill. On line Networking for beginners is still very new and therefor there are many mistakes to be made and ideas to be learned from the practice. The inherent flaw with networking on line comes from the beginning of the Internet and we must understand the beginning to understand where we can go and how to get there.

The inherent flaw of networking on line is that as the Internet revolution took off, it became a way for people to be dishonest and hide while they have done horrible things to unsuspecting people on the Internet. The Internet was seen as a scary place as strangers enter into your home or work place and seek to do you harm. They try and scam you out of money, take your information or perform other types of harm all the while by hiding behind a fake name and profile.

That was before the last couple of years when people started to figure out there were something much bigger to be gained on line. More money and riches without the illegal activity and being scared of who you are dealing with is going away rapidly. They discovered what is called building a platform or building up your name and reputation on line. This makes networking on line possible and powerful.

In today's world, since we now are concerned with building our reputation and name on line, we have the best chance ever of getting to know each other and helping each other to build our businesses on line. The Internet still may be a bit scary, but overall it has become a whole lot better to deal with. It holds a plethora of opportunity for networkers who wish to build relationships all over the world.

Building relationships on line needs to be treated just like that BNI meeting that I described. You need to be structured and accountable for your actions. You need to have daily operations and follow some rules. You need to schedule virtual coffee meetings. Relationship building needs to be a high priority and the ability to build quality relationships is more than possible.

If you are one who likes to look people in the eye then you can use video or pictures, webinars or social media. Do not let the fact that you are not belly to belly with your business connections sway you from networking on line.

So the first step to getting started is by simply starting conversations with people. I am sure you are on Facebook, twitter or Pinterest and I am sure you have some friends or connections. Now, we are going to start to build business connections with your social media accounts and the forums you go on and the video sites and more. You have the biggest opportunity ever today to build a ton of meaningful business connections.

Once you get the conversations started, step two is to look for ways to help your fellow connections. Almost everything applies in the real world of networking as it does on the on line world of networking. Step three is to build your business.

13.2. How to Maintain Your Networking Relationships

Starting a relationship both on line and off line is the easy part. Maintaining those relationships is a much bigger and tougher task. In order for you to become successful you need to understand how to maintain your relationships. You see, you really are only capable of maintaining so many relationships at a time. The key is to rotate them so that you can properly get in front of them on a regular basis.

As a human being, you only have so many hours in the day. If you have an organization, then you can delegate some of the tasks of maintaining relationships but if you are a one person business then you will have to work on a system to make sure that you are building your business with your contacts.

On an average let's say you can properly maintain ten relationships at a time responsibly but you have over 100 contacts. What do you do about the other ninety? The answer really is simple; we deal with ten at a time. You will have to rotate your time and relationship building in a major way while you deal with the rest in a minor way.

For the ten you are currently servicing, we will get in front of these people with coffee meetings, lunches, office visits, phone calls, email etc. We will go all out until we get to the point where we have something substantial. You must be genuine and resist the temptation to cram your time. This is not about building shallow relationships and faking your time together. This is about building in quality into your relationships ten people at a time.

How long you spend building up each group will depend on your efficiency. What you will have to make sure you keep in mind is that you have to service everyone in some way or the connection may drift away. What you need are constant small touches to everyone, while you make bigger impacts with each group of ten. This is much like a juggling act. Loose focus and you will drop the ball somewhere.

I cannot stress enough the keeping files on your prospects and clients are very important. Since you are rotating your attention, you will need a data base of some sort to make sure you never skip a beat. Professionals will keep exact notes and amateurs will try and commit everything to mind. This would be a huge mistake and the consequences will be lost connections.

How do we build relationships? We spend time with those people we want to get to know and it is no different with business relationships. You will have to commit to the process and be very serious about what you are doing. Going after building relationships with clients and not being sincere is obvious to everyone so make sure you want to be great at networking.

When you start the process of networking, you are starting the process of relationship building. Have fun with the process and enjoy the people you are getting to know. You are about to discover the incredible power of what building relationships in business can do for your business.

13.3. Do You Have to Buy From the Group?

When I help people learn how to network and join groups, I am often asked once they join, "what do I do if I do not want to use certain people in the group?" This is a tough question as you have joined a group to help each other grow and network resources together. You are supposed to build a bond with your fellow members and buy from them when services or products like theirs are needed. The problem is what do you do if they are not good service providers, have bad products or are just not plain good people?

First of all I always suggest holding back in the beginning with everyone. I do not mean don't participate, but I do mean don't hang your neck out too far until you have spent some time with them and have started to understand their business practices. Get to know how they handle issues and how they speak to people.

You need to observe them from a safe distance and invest the time to know who you are doing business with. All networkers are not created equal and just because they have been in this group for a long time does not make them a great person to do business with. I'll give you an example of what I am talking about.

I had joined this group that I thought I wanted to put some of my valuable time into to help grow my business. I thought I had checked it out well and that I had made a wise decision but at the end of the day I was wrong. In order to understand a group, you must understand its leadership.

This group I attended had an area director in it that was very controlling and biased. She liked those who she could control and that would not fight her or speak up. There were a handful of people who had been in the group long term and after getting to know them I understood how they had lasted so long not doing their part.

These members were horrible with their customer service, attitude and their elected power. I could not refer business to them and the one I did refer business too I was sorry that I did. He never returned phone calls, never followed through and was extremely difficult to deal with in all aspects. This was a small sampling of people in the group but I did not have it in my heart to do business with them or pass business to them. It is my right and I decide whom I do business with at all times.

You have the same right and you do not have to announce it either. If you decide to schedule meetings with people and get to know them, then I think that is a great idea. I suggest being honest to the individual if you like or just smile and act cordial. You really do not have to declare anything as you never know what could happen. Down the road you might end up building a solid relationship with this person and doing a lot of business together. That did not happen in my case and ultimately I left that particular group. It was more than a one or two member problem as it was a leadership problem that trickled down.

You should try your best to build relationships with other members and help them grow your business. No matter if you use them for services or refer others to them, you need to be comfortable the whole time with these scenarios. Never feel pressured and always take the time to get to know and understand them as your business is depending on it.

13.4. Figuring Out Personalities

One of the most important skills in business is listening and the second most important skill is observing. These two skills can serve any business owner well in growing their business. When we are talking about networking and leveraging people we need to build relationships and because of that, we need to figure out the personalities of people in the group. This will prove to be very valuable as you plan your business tactics and relationships as you spend more time with the group. Business is about planning and relationships' planning is paramount.

This is not a chapter on personality types or coming up with new names for people and how they act. This is a simple understanding of the people you will find in networking groups and who they are as people. No matter if people are good or bad, we need to understand them so we can understand if they will be of help or not. There may be rules that everyone is supposed to follow but do not be fooled as some people just do not conform or consider others.

In the group you will come across what I call the serial networker. This is just a label I use but this type of person has been hanging around networking for many years. A few are still very upbeat while others are soured. They can be very good for connections but may not be so helpful to do business with. They will probably be the most skeptical as they have seen a lot during their tenure. Trying to be overly enthusiastic with these people is usually a mistake as they have been hardened by all of the people whom have come and gone.

Then you have the new comers who are just like you. They are new, eager and have all kinds of ideas. They are eager to share and fit in and will try and either goes out of their way to help you or they will be too busy taking. New comers do not necessarily understand the idea of giving or how the group works. You should proceed with caution and work with these people like a new volunteer. Be smart but know they are not paid professionals.

Then you have the professional networkers who have been around a while, are not so soured and are optimistic. These people can and will help you the most. They have the personality of entrepreneurs who understand why they are at networking and how to help both you and them at the same time. They are eager to build their business but will not jeopardize their professional status in any way. They will carry themselves well and are often very outgoing. Clicks are not as important to them as building quality relationships are. Look for the professional networker that you can partner with a really build great relationships.

There are other personalities to figure out along the way like the visitor for instance. These are often times tire kickers who are there to see what is in it for them. Not all visitors are tire kickers or takers, but a good portion is clueless about great networking. The act of giving in order to receive is often foreign to most visitors or first time networkers. There are also the officers or leaders of the group you need to learn about. Some of these are there for cheap power and recognition while others want to truly help. Try and figure out the personalities of the group and you will become very successful quickly.

Robert D. Kintigh

14. Leadership in Networking

I would love to tell you that the people running the group you joined or are visiting are the best leaders in the group, but often times this is not the case. Leadership in networking is no different than most companies, groups or organizations today; people get put up in front of the room for many reasons and good leadership is not always the case.

Do not assume that the person up in front of the room is the leader of the group and do not assume that you can follow their lead. Leadership in networking is seriously lacking and if anyone is going to get your loyalty then they should have to earn it. You must always interview someone for the job of leader and make sure that they deserve your attention and respect. There are many great leaders in networking and all I am saying is to pay attention for your own sake.

What is the job of leadership in networking? In my opinion I believe that the leadership in networking should start with making sure that everyone is educated and feels comfortable. They need to reach out to everyone in the group and make sure that no one is left stranded or clueless as to how they should act or work within the group.

Leadership in networking should also include the way people communicate during meetings, one to one meetings, in their business and in other group activities. Poor communication is the sign of a poor leader. You must get good at the art of communication to be a great leader.

Great leadership also shows through on how you run your business and when you are a poor leader how you do things will tell the tale of your leadership. Let me give you an example in the hopes that you will get my point.

If you are in networking and you are the President of the group or the treasurer or hold any business, I would hope that you set an example for the rest of the group. If you are not capable then you should not hold a seat or leadership position.

The purpose of being in the group is to grow your business and have others refer business to you and nothing takes away the confidence of this more than having poor business practices. An example would be not returning phone calls in a timely manner or having others come to your office to see your desk that looks like a bomb blew up.

This is a true story and it is hard to respect someone who operates like this. Everything you do is seen by others in the group. The same thing goes for your home or office. Do not have others from the group come over to your home or office if it is a disaster or in bad shape. You are projecting an image to others by what you represent.

Leadership is a responsibility and is also a teaching tool. How you run things in the group will show your true strength and character. Make sure that you understand the consequences of your actions and never negate your responsibilities as a leader. I have seen too often that poor choices are made by leaders in networking and they are never corrected.

Great leadership is never afraid to admit that poor choices were made and then an attempt is made to correct these mistakes. Poor leaders will stick to their guns and go down with the ship. This mentality is wrong and hurts the group as a whole. When decisions are made, they need to be made with the group in mind and not one or two people.

Your responsibility as a leader in the group is bigger than you and needs to be treated accordingly so that you give the group the best chance possible to grow.

14.1. The Difference between Networking and Marketing

Have you ever asked yourself what is the difference between networking and marketing? They really are two different acts and ideas. You own a business and you want to grow it and you need different tools to accomplish the task.

Much like a builder needs several tools to build a house. A hammer only goes so far in the process and other tools are brought in. Networking is another tool and is not the best tool or the worst tool; it is just another important tool to building a business.

Balancing Between Networking and Working Your Business is very important to understand and work on. They are the same and totally different. Networking is the practice of building relationships in the hopes that the relationships will turn into business and that will equate to profits.

Networking is not walking around with a bull horn screaming about your business. Networking is taking the time to let others get to know about you and who you are in order to want to pass business to you.

Networking is all about educating others about your products or services and what are the values and benefits to doing business with you. You educate your sales force on everything you have to offer and how you are going to help their connections. If you are not educating others about who you are and what your company does then they will struggle to pass you referrals.

When you meet with another member you both have a job to do and that job is often taken casually. Focus in and learn about them as much as you can and then teach them about you. Details are important and making sure you get your business the attention it deserves is very important.

While you are networking you are building relationships. While you are marketing, you are building awareness about your business. Marketing is the act of planning and executing and is not to be confused with advertising. Marketing your business is about informing the general public about your business. You are telling the world that you are what you do and where you can be found.

You will network and market together at times. For instance we held a gold tournament through our networking group and I had marketing materials and sponsored during the tournament to market my business.

The reason to point out the differences between the two is because people will often visit a networking group or even join one and then they spend the whole time marketing their business. You can do this on your own and the group is then not needed.

You want to join networking to build relationships that will go out and market your business for you. They will become your walking/talking commercials but only after they get you and who you are and what you are about.

I hope you now understand the difference between the two and what I am trying to make clear. Be responsible with networking and do not scream at people all about your company but yet you must educate them about your company. Make it a casual conversation that is thorough and clear.

Think of it as orientation day every chance you get to sit down with someone and let your sales force know what they need to know in order to be successful in building the company and their paycheck. Your fellow members want to make sure you are successful as it helps them to become successful too!

14.2. How to Approach the People in the Networking Group

In previous chapters we talked about how to figure out personalities so we understand the best people to help us build our business. This is a little about personalities but is more about how to approach people in the group so that you can benefit from their circle of connections. If we approach people in the wrong way then we will lesson our chances of building an outrageous business through the group.

Remember that we are dealing with personalities here and all people are individuals. I have yet to meet the same person twice and because of that everyone needs to be treated like an individual. This may be one of the biggest mistakes people make in business. They try and cookie cutter everyone and treat everyone the same. Your approach must be unique to the person.

I hear it all the time that people do not want to deal with him on his terms or her terms but isn't this what we should be doing in many cases in life? Shouldn't we deal with people on their terms? After all, people are who they are and tell you how they like it if you will listen.

Some members of the group will be very open, outgoing and welcome you any time. These people who often seem cheery and happy are often times tough to get them to focus. That very bubbly and big smiley face might be the bane of existence so the approach with them will have to be a combination of upbeat and serious.

The hardened, serious people of the group will have to be approached often times from the perspective of their knowledge and personality. These are not people to approach with lots of humor and laughter but with serious business on your mind.

There are too many types to list as I stated above about people being individuals but I think you get the idea. Think about things before you do them and your success will increase rapidly. I love to watch and observe people and can do it for hours. It is an acquired skill but one that pays off heavily. You need to observe people to really get a feeling for who they are and their mannerisms.

On the approach with people I try to never assume anything. I go into meeting people with as much of an open mind as possible. I love using questions to get to know and understand them. Let them decide who they are and let them paint the picture. It is so much easier to be open minded than to have to change your mind later.

In networking you will get many chances to learn how to approach people as you will meet many new people along the way. Learn to become proficient at it and perfect the approach. Maybe this is a dying art and the youth of today is not interested in things like this, but I hope that it catches back on.

I would not consider myself old or young as I am in the middle but I feel like sometimes I am really old when I think about these types of values. Shaking hands, looking people in the eyes, how you walk, how you talk all used to be important things.

Today, the younger generation has no clue about things like the approach as long as the video game controller works or the cyber camera. For the rest of us professionals out there, I hope you work on your skills of humanity.

14.3. Learn How to Help Your Members

It was over 15 years ago when I was sitting in a seminar and the speaker asked if anyone knew the secret to creating an outrageously successful business. A few said yes but most people didn't say a word. They were there to find out the secret to having this occur. I was intrigued and was awaiting the answer to his question. I was thinking about building factories and finding gold, hiring a thousand people or inventing something new. His answer threw me for about 20 minutes.

The speaker said that the answer to riches through your business or profession was a simple one and was something that could be mastered. It did not take a genius or some new invention; there was no gold needed or an army of people at work to accomplish it.

I was now at full attention and listening closely. He said if you truly want to prosper and make all of the money in the world, all you have to do is learn to help people. He said I could leave you with this one thought alone and you would be set for the rest of your life. There were 5 more hours to his seminar so he continued but he had made his impact on me.

I have to admit I was stunned for a while as he delivered his answer and I sat there milling over what he was talking about. He went on to fully explain himself and as I took notes and the impact was felt deeper I totally got it. Help yourself and get by. If you help others then you will go a long way. What he was talking about was finding ways to solve people's problems or at least problems that you could help solve.

He wasn't talking about curing cancer or building a house for people unless you could afford that. What he was talking about was solving things that people could not do easily on their own. It might be to help with their charity, find people or resources to help them, connect them with other professionals or save them money on something they used. These are all things that are easy enough to do if we pay attention.

If you read enough of what I write, you will quickly learn that I have taken this to heart and it has become a very strong tool to building my businesses long term. I love to help people and the return has been tremendous. You might ask if it has never paid itself back and the answer would be yes.

There has been more times than I can remember when I helped someone and they never even gave me a thank you let along returned any favors or business. This is okay and you need to feel that way too because you are in it to win and winning is a big picture. To think you will ever get a 100 percent return on anything is ridiculous but the return on this strategy is the highest of anything I have done in business.

If there was one thing I could give you to change your business and life it would be to teach you to help others. All too often I have found most business owners are selfish and if we can get more to focus on helping others. Imagine our world if we can get this idea around like it should be. The business world would never be the same. We can help to get it out there in a bigger way.

Small Business Marketing 101

15. Your Business and Networking

If your business has been lagging behind the last couple of years and you are looking for a way to increase sales and profits, then my suggestion is for you to engage in networking both on line and off line. There are world of benefits to engaging in networking and your business can enjoy an increase in prospects. Here are just some of the benefits to networking for your business:

- Increase awareness of your business
- A volunteer sales force
- Expanded resources for your business
- Willingness of others to help you build your business
- Sounding boards for your ideas
- Gives you a way to give back to others
- Increased education
- A better focus
- More credibility
- Lasting relationships

Your business needs networking to grow at a rapid rate. The increased awareness of your business pays huge dividends farther than you can imagine because you never know who will pull out your business card or tell a colleague or client about your business. As your circle of influence continues to grow so will your business and learning how valuable networking is will greatly serve you and your business.

More credibility is very powerful and you should think about it much like the rating system on Amazon or Ebay. Your networking members help you with credibility and that helps to ease people and their tension over using your services or products. We all love to buy but when we can get confirmation that something is good or viable then we feel so much better.

A better focus because you stop thinking only about your business and you start to relax as you focus on helping others. Your thinking will alter and you will take things to a different level. You can't help yourself but to think differently. You must pop your head up and look around and listen. The mentality is incredibly different and much more rewarding.

An all-volunteer sales force ready to help you and your business. When in your life have you ever had this happen for your business? If you have never experienced this before you are in for a real treat. Treat your fellow members' right so they are quick to pull out your name to a prospect. What you are always looking for from your fellow networkers is that warm introduction.

You need to and want to feel like a known entity. You want people to relax as soon as possible so that you can focus on what you can do for them and why you are the right solution. Be thankful for your members as they will work hard for you and get your foot in the door.

15.1. The Basics of Online Networking

On line networking is an entire subject on its own and could be an entire book if not many. This is not a book of A to Z instructions of everything to do with on line networking. For the purpose of what I am trying to teach you, the correspondence of on line networking to real world networking is to draw a complete picture for you of where to find warm leads, how to secure them and how to use them to grow your business.

Let's start with common sense when it comes to networking on line. We must always do the basics first and perfect that in order to do some of the advanced things. As much as it seems a given I want you to start with being as nice as you can to everyone you come across on line. There are many people on line that are not so nice and would love to focus on causing you harm just to be mean person. So a good rule of thumb is to be nice at all cost.

Second, get to know who you are dealing with. Take your time and build a real foundation. In my mind on line consist of chat, video, pictures, information, and even the telephone. Be patient and get to know these new on line networkers and make sure you want to do business with them.

Just like in person networking you should make sure you always do your part. I caution you not to be a taker when you are networking your business online. Remember the BNI motto a Givers gain? Be a giver and not a taker and you will gain all that you need.

Look for ways to help your on line networkers. They need help and you need help and you can do it the same way you do in person. Just pay attention, keep your eyes and ears open and ask questions to figure out how to help. If you build any kind of relationship with people on line they will tell you what you need to know just like the person sitting across from you at a one to one.

Be cautious but not paranoid as you want to build relationships and if you do not trust people then that is exactly what you will get. The basis for networking is building trust and sharing. On line we call it cooperative marketing. The idea behind it is to take away the worry about the two of you cross promoting or marketing for each other without competition. Do not be foolish but yet don't blow a relationship that can develop into something bigger.

Do a Google, Bing and Yahoo search and do your homework on your new networking relationship. One of the strengths of marketing and using on line is the fact that you can investigate what someone is up to and without fear of them knowing that you are doing it.

Everything on line is not gospel or necessarily factual but people do leave clues and patters you might be able to pick up on. At minimum you can have some questions or have some kind of background on someone. For instance, start with Googling me and see what you can learn.

The basics to networking on line are very important and can help your business grow. Any coach will always tell you that mastering the basics win championships. Networking on line is no different and if you will spend the time to master the basics of networking on line, then you will do very well in finding quality relationships.

15.2. Practice Makes Perfect – Perfecting Social Skills

Social skills in networking are paramount to achieving success and it takes practice as networking is a skill to be learned. It is not about sitting around socializing or taking. It is not about coffee meetings and cocktails after hours. It is the act of building relationships and your business and the better your social skills are the better chance you will have to get them to buy from you.

If you are this far in the book then you have read through many of my suggestions and a lot of them have to do with the way you deal with people especially in networking. I hope by now you understand the mental aspects of what you need to do in networking. I have highlighted many aspects to the mental game of networking as it is extremely important to your success. Use the techniques I have included to begin your networking journey.

You will never be perfect as you learn networking. You may even enjoy it for years so do not get yourself worked up when you slip up. What we really need to work on is the pursuit of perfection and work on our skills every day. You should never let down even a day because there is so much to learn and work on. I do not believe in doing anything half-way as it is not worth the time. Let's attack the art of networking and realize big profits from your hard work.

One of the techniques I like to use in perfecting my skills is I like to use video to see how I speak, look at my body language and my gestures. It may seem a little weird but I assure you that it is not. These are the things that professionals do to perform better. Also, work on getting better at video period because if you are going to be effective on line, then you need to improve your appearance and genuineness. You need to work on coming across video as believable and honest and unfortunately that takes practice. You also want to look credible and a great fit for the networking prospect.

I also use recipe cards to write down questions and then I work on putting them into conversational form. When you are investigating and gathering facts, they need to come out as conversational as possible. Look in a mirror and practice your elevator speech and observe your body language and facial expressions. I also like using the mirror to practice my smile. A smile is very powerful in life and networking.

There are so many things you can perfect or at least the pursuit thereof and I suggest that you do. Like most things, networking in the top 10% of businesses out there is not tough to crack. If you put in the extra work, you will be surprised how quickly you end up in the top of all networkers both on and off line.

15.3. Ready, Set, Go – Network!

So to get started you should work on your 30 second commercial and work on it till it flows and sounds professional. Next you should map out your networking meetings to visit and book them out in your outlook or calendar. Next, find the coffee shops or Panera Breads or meeting places near the networking. Then get ready to work hard and have fun building your business. Happy Networking!

16. The Mobile App Revolution for Small Business

Welcome to the revolution that is taking place! If you are here reading this book then perhaps you have figured out that there is a major movement or revolution happening called the mobile app revolution. This industry is already so big that the mobile app industry has already been responsible for approximately 500,000 new jobs since 2007. This is amazing for an industry that wasn't even in existence before that year.

There is also something else that is happening that makes that industry so robust and exciting and that is the explosion of sales of smart phones and tablets. These devices are being sold by the millions monthly and for the first time that I can remember in history is being coveted by both the young and old users. A piece of technology called the smart phone or tablet that is captivating both of these demographics in a way like never before.

We are calling it a mobile app revolution for small business because the mobile app is in a time period where the small business can finally afford it and harness its power thanks to the advancement of technology and the help of a company called Genepoch.

We are writing this book so that you will be well informed as a small business about the possibilities and capabilities of a mobile app. It is time that you not only know what a mobile app is, but what the mobile app can do for your small business and what it is going to take to help get your business found on the go.

This book is dedicated to straight forward information for you and your business and what is all involved in the industry. We are going to present to you some facts and statistics, tips, marketing ideas and options for your small business to either design, deploy and publish your app, have someone assist you or have a custom app built for you with your guidance.

You do not have to be afraid of this new technology and you should definitely not dismiss it because you don't understand it. As a small business owner it is your responsibility to help your small business any way you can and unfortunately that often takes learning new things and implementing new strategies. Learning this new strategy and marketing medium is not going to take you long to understand the following information or value:

- What is a mobile app
- How to market a mobile app
- What is the cost of a mobile app
- What are the elements to an effective mobile app
- What is the potential R.O.I. of a mobile app
- Why it is a must to have a mobile app
- How a mobile app works
- How the app stores work
- What option is best for you to get a mobile app
- Best practices for building a mobile app
- What you want in your mobile app
- Powerful features available
- What is PNS
- Why text message marketing just doesn't compete

What we would like you to learn from the beginning is why you need and must have a mobile app and what is driving this demand. Did you know that mobile apps have been downloaded over 25 Billion times to date and the mobile device is outpacing the desktop by 94 minutes a day? Lastly, 91% of all smart phone users in the United States have their mobile device within reach 24 hours a day. This should give you some powerful thoughts right off the back what this book is going to lay out for you about why you must get a mobile application right away for your business.

As you continue on reading, get ready to be amazed and intrigued by all of the wonderful information it possess about the mobile app industry. We hope that you will ultimately decide to get a mobile app and that you will trust our firm and mobile app platform to help you accomplish your goals. Even if you do not choose one of our options, we hope that you do not delay and that we have delivered information that will help you to get comfortable with this new technology and that you will understand the benefits and values. This technology is here to stay and your business is in the perfect position to benefit from it.

16.1. Introducing the Mobile App

You may or may not realize what I mean by getting your small business a mobile app. The business mobile app is like one of those tiny app icons on your smart phone or tablet that I am sure you have downloaded and played with to some small or large degree. You can get an app similar to your favorite restaurant, retail store, JcPenny or Fandango for movie tickets.

A mobile app in its simplistic form is a tiny bundle (app icon) that people download to their device so that they can get all of your company information and offerings in one place; like your social media, website, directions, phone and email, e commerce and a call to action all in one neat download. No more searching around all over the web to make a buying decision. The file is not bulky on your phone and the user has a great experience when deciding to do business with your company.

A mobile app should really be a call to action or a reason prospects and customers should take action with your company. An example of this might be that you will give one free entrée with the purchase of another if they come in Tuesday nights. A call to action on your mobile app is paramount and one of the best things you can use a mobile app for in my opinion. We will talk about important elements of your mobile app as we move on, but I wanted to start to formulate ideas in your mind so you can begin to plan ideas for your mobile app.

The mobile app has become popular because they are resized to work with the mobile device you are using. No more taking your finger and scrolling all over the place. You know what I mean, right? Right now if you use your browser on your device and you look up a business's website it pulls up and the *"mobile friendly website"* is too big for the screen. What you have to do is drag the screen all around to find what you need. This is not a good user experience and this is what we need to shoot for as a business offering a mobile experience. If you do not offer that great mobile experience then you will risk losing prospects to your competition.

There are many great features that you can add to your mobile app to help your prospects and customers. There are also easy to use features to communicate, get social with and share with people. A mobile app is now as important as a website and really has become more important than a website due to the nature of the ever expanding network of smart devices.

You want to go true mobile today because people all over the world now have the best of both worlds. They get to go wherever they want and they get to bring their favorite computing devices with them. They are no longer strapped behind their desks limited by the view that they see out their window. They get to go out and experience the world all the while they get to stay connected and find their favorite businesses and information. For the last couple of years the mobile app has been enjoyed by bigger businesses as the average cost is way more than the small business can stomach. This is no longer the case.

As you continue to discover more about the importance of mobile apps, we are going to lay the foundation for what your mobile app should do, how it should look, how it should function and what it is going to take to get it on Apple. We will explain about the app stores and how you can market your app and get reviews for it.

We will do everything in our power to give you all of the information that you need to make a smart purchasing decision and not walk away from one of the most powerful marketing pieces to come about in the last 100 years. You need a mobile app and you must have a mobile app to compete in the new world of smart devices. So get ready to learn all about what the mobile app is about and how you are going to profit from it.

Lastly, this book covers many aspects of how you can or will get your mobile app developed. We talk about the services offered by our firm, utilizing the mobile app platform GenEpoch which also includes utilizing the self-design and build option. What we are most interested in accomplishing with this book is helping to make more people and small businesses aware of the mobile app and the low cost options that are available to them as so many people still do not know about them. We understand that you may also have someone else build your app and that is okay, but at least you will know what you should expect from them in their performance and execution.

16.2. Why You Should Utilize a Platform for Developing Your Mobile App

Businesses today (2012-2013) spend an average of $6000 dollars just to develop a mobile app and then hundreds and sometimes thousands more to keep their app content updated.
The cost to develop, deploy and maintain a mobile app for most businesses is too expensive, complicated and takes a great deal of time, until Now!

If you decide that you want to design and deploy your own mobile app or if you decide to have us design your mobile app, then you will be utilizing the most powerful mobile app platform available by Genepoch (www.joingenepoch.com) This mobile app developer platform has features that you just can't find anywhere. Let's take a look this company called Genepoch and why what they have accomplished in the industry helps your small business.

Founded in 2011, GenEpoch which is located in Walnut Creek California and is a debt-free company with thousands of active customers using its technology today. The landscape has been forever changed for small businesses and entrepreneurs who are looking to have a mobile presence for their business. You see, the founders of the company envisioned a technology that makes it easy for anyone to have a mobile presence that requires very little effort to design, maintain, that is affordable and more importantly....an immediate return on investment. In addition, the technology had to work across a broad range of mobile devices, such as iPhone, iPad, Android and the mobile web.

They also insisted that this technology be brought to small businesses through a network of entrepreneurs all throughout the United States. By the way, their technology has been featured in several major media outlets. Now that you have a better understanding from where GenEpoch was founded, let's learn more about features, pricing and important aspects to make your company come alive on the mobile device.

16.3. Custom Graphics on Your Mobile App

The difference between a run-of-the-mill mobile app and a dynamic mobile app is the graphics. When building and designing a mobile app on a platform, you will find that you will need a graphic on most of the backgrounds. To create a dynamic and powerful mobile app, you will want to be sure to include custom graphics that are high resolution and professional in design. This is essential in extending your brand as you want to look your best. This will also be very important when trying to publish your app to the App Store. Apple looks for very clean, high resolution images that give a great presentation. If you are building your own app on a platform and you do not know graphic work, I would suggest hiring a company to help you with all your graphics. First impressions are very important so do not cheat a very valuable piece of your companies look and brand.

When adding graphics to your app, follow these simple tips to help you build and design an amazing mobile app that will get you the exposure you are looking for:

- Use only high res images throughout the entire mobile app. The worst thing you can do is having distorted or pixelated images on a mobile app that represents your business or company. Mobile app impressions are everything to the app user.

- Be sure to follow guidelines on a mobile app platform and App Store as to what size screen shots and icons to upload. In the platform we currently use it calls for 640x840 mobile size screen shots and 960x1260 iPad screen shots. You are now able to upload iPhone5 screen shots which require 640x1136 sized shots. As for the icon, you will find this requires to be sized at 512x512. Keeping the correct dimensions is very important when building a mobile app.

- Do not create busy or cluttered backgrounds. Keep your backgrounds clean, professional, and neat. If you make your images too busy it will distract from what you are trying to display on your app. This is just a basic rule we go by. I find that on the ios tabs or features, I keep the background white and find a nice colorful image to display on the bottom half of the screen. See below for examples of a newsletter feature:

- Do not steal images off of Google as most of those are copyrighted or you do not have rights to use them. You want to use your own photos that you have rights to legally. You can also buy your images from a stock photo site. Two very affordable stock photo sites you can try out are: Depositphotos and Dreamstime. These are royalty free photos and images you can use. They also have a section of free images you can use under your account name. Stock photos are a great way to enhance your mobile app.

- Be sure to keep your mobile app within a color scheme as you design. When building apps for clients, we like to choose two to three main colors that we incorporate throughout the entire app. You want your mobile app to flow. Too many colors will only distract the app user and maybe even turn them away. Not only do you want to keep all of your graphic work within the color scheme, but you also want your menu bars, headers, and inner buttons to be within the color scheme as well. See screen shots below where we have followed this rule to ensure the colors flow from one screen to another:

• Choose your typeface and font carefully when designing your graphics. You want your font to match the feel of your mobile app. You always want to use fonts that are readable but yet are fun to use in designs. Some of our favorite typefaces to use on mobile apps: **Myriad Pro** (it's a sans serif and is comfortable to read and it's a great choice to use in typography). Another one is **Weston** (this is a new slab-serif font that is suitable for logos and headlines. It's a different font to use and will spice up your designs.) **Monotype Corsiva** is a script typeface that is a style of the early Italian cursives.

• This is a great font to use for taglines to add some interest to your design. **Chunkfive** (solid heavy font that makes a statement. Great for headlines). Some other typefaces we love using in our designs: **Corbel, Monika, Century Gothic, futura, League Gothic, Franchise, and Franklin Gothic**. You can experiment yourself with different typefaces and fonts to find what you like using in your mobile app designs.

Less is better. If you are not sure what to design at any point, just go simple as less is always better on a mobile app. The purpose of a business mobile app is to keep the experience simple so the user can easily navigate through the app. If you want to play it safe when designing, just remember "less is better". Look at how you are designing your mobile app from a third party view point and be as objective as possible. While designing get several eyes on your graphics and make sure they are appealing.

16.4. Building and Designing Your Mobile App – Low Cost Option

Using the Mobile App Platform Located At:
www.JoinGenEpoch.com

The mobile app platform (MAP) allows small businesses to build their own app at a more affordable price and in a short period of time. With the MAP, small businesses can have full control of the content and design that goes into their app. With the MAP there is no need for programming knowledge. There are many features that easily integrate into your mobile app. The MAP makes it easy for anyone to design, publish, and maintain a mobile app 24/7 online. After you build and design your mobile app you can have it published to the Apple and Google app stores.

The MAP has five modules: functionality, content, appearance, preview, and publish.

Functionality: this is where you add your features also known as tabs. In this module you can name your tabs and choose an icon.

Content: in this module you are taking each tab and adding the required information such as your business description, events, promotions, contact info, photo gallery and so on. It's easy as just pointing and clicking on a tab and filling it out the way you desire.

Appearance: this is where you will choose how you want your mobile app to look and feel. You can customize the layout with a classic or premium style, customize buttons, customize color theme, choose your style of icons, and upload background images.

Preview: this module is available anytime during your mobile app building process so that you can preview your app and get a better idea of what it will look like on a mobile device.

Publish: this module is where you will finalize the mobile app process by filling in your mobile app name, description, keywords, functions, screenshots, and icon. After you complete this module you will then send over your app to the review team at Genepoch so that they can make sure your app is ready to send over to the Apple App Store.

Important Elements to Remember When Building Your App:

1. Be sure to start by adding your website url in the dashboard. MAP will pull information from your site that will help you in getting your app started. By adding your url, MAP will also mobilize your website. You then will need to create more features or tabs that you want to add in the functionality module.

2. When choosing the features or tabs to use in your mobile app, there are some important points to remember when doing this. These points are only to help in making it easier for you to be able to publish to the Apple App Store. These points are as follows:

a. Utilize tabs in your app that use iPhone native functionality. Tabs that use native functionality include: Home, Contact Tab, Email Photo tab, Messages tab (push notifications), QR Coupon tab, GPS Coupon tab, and Fan Wall tab.

b. Do not use more than three info tabs and no more than three website tabs.

c. Use a minimum of ten tabs but no more than fifteen. You want enough information on your   app to make it interesting enough for people to want to download but you don't want too much information to make it look like a website.

3. Keep your mobile app simple (bare essentials) when sending over to the Apple App Store for review. After your app is approved you can then add or change any of the features or tabs. Keeping your app simple is your best bet in getting it approved by Apple.

4. Only add features that relate to your industry. For example: if you are an author or consultant, it's not necessary to have a tip calculator tab on your app. You want features that will help your purpose and engage the app user.

5. Be sure to add attractive background images to all of your ios features; apps with a dynamic appearance will get more exposure in the app store. App impressions are everything!

6. Be sure to add these great app features as these are some of our favorites and some are necessary to getting your mobile app published: Home Tab, Contact Tab, Subscribe, Push Notifications (messages tab), Email Photo Tab, Fan Wall, Gallery, GPS, voice notes, and Tell Friend. Every business can use these specific features or tabs on their mobile app. These are the kind of features that Apple likes to see on mobile apps. You should be good if you use at least 5 of these features and add your own business tabs for the remainder that relate to your industry. Example of other features or tabs to use: shop, about us, social media, services, free quote, coupon, blog, website, events, menu, contest, and so on....

7. Use high resolution images throughout your app as this will be the first things app users will notice. Having clean and professional images will make or break your mobile app. The biggest turn off: a user goes onto a mobile app and sees distorted or pixelated images. Apple app store will also reject your app for not having a nice presentation. If you are not able to design your mobile app with a nice appearance then you should consult with a marketing and design company such as SCM Web_Team (www.scmwebteam.com)who specialize in building and designing mobile apps and graphic design. Also see our section about custom graphics for more detail.

8. Add quality content to your app. Add original content that will attract your users. Check your content for spelling, grammatical, typographical and factual errors before submitting to the App Store. Dynamic appearance and quality content will go a long way.

9. Be sure your mobile app has a purpose and functionality. You want to add features and content that gives your app the purpose you

are looking for. Keep in mind while building your app; you want to add function that will keep your users coming back for more.

10. Choosing your mobile app name and keywords are important to your app's success in the marketplace. Your app name besides the icon is the first thing potential users will see when browsing apps. For business apps, be descriptive as you can from the beginning so your app is recognizable for what it really is. You want to choose a name that identifies with your mobile app's functions.

As for keywords, you want to choose wisely. Use the key phrases you want your mobile app to be found under. Be sure to separate your keywords in the App Store with a comma. When adding your keywords make sure it's not something that is overused as you can try adding synonyms or other phrases that you think people will use to search your mobile app. Do not be too general when adding keywords, for example; you may not want to use "restaurant" as that is very general, instead try adding "pizza restaurant". A great tool to use to test your keywords is Appcod.es and you can also see what your competitors are using for keywords.

11. Help your app stand out from the competition by writing a good description of what your app is about. The description is a very important tool in helping you promote your app as well as getting it approved on the App Store. Be sure to describe or list your app's functions so potential users know what to expect.

Robert D. Kintigh

17. Mobile App Versus a Website

People are always asking me if they should get a mobile app or a website or both, which tells me that they do not understand the concept of a mobile app quite yet. If you are looking to have people find you on the Internet and you do not have a website or social media site then you will probably not get found. This holds true for mobile marketing as well for you. If you don't have a mobile app then the likely hood of you being found on one of the app stores or mobile on line is impossible.

There are some similarities between a website and a mobile app, but there are some that appear similar and are not. For instance, a mobile app is not a heavy piece of marketing like a website is. You do not build out a hundred page mobile app like you would a website. The more tabs you have does not equate to better SEO. The mobile app store is set up based upon keywords and category. A mobile app should be clean and to the point and not heavy with information. If you load up your mobile app with too much information or tabs then people will not have a great experience while visiting your app.

A website might be able to get away with a poor look or low grade graphics, but not a mobile app especially on Apple. Your customers especially will not forgive a poorly constructed app where as an ugly website can still generate traffic and profits. There is not a lot behind the scenes on a mobile app like a website does.

The purpose of a website is to go out and grab traffic on the Internet. The main purpose of a mobile app is to create loyalty and improve communications with mobile prospects and customers. You might decide that you do not need a mobile app and to that we will say that you just cut out about 60% of your potential market. This revolution is happening with or without you and the biggest mistake you can make is to not participate.

This really isn't a question of one or another. The mobile app and a website can and should work together. You will link your website to your mobile app and you should link your website to your mobile app. When you are marketing a business, you need to use everything at your disposal and you should start with the most powerful pieces. The main aspect to finding people is to go where they are located and the mobile app and website have those people.

17.1. How Social Media Comes Into Play

Like I said before, your mobile app is like a neat package that houses all of your company's offerings. Your mobile app to your website to your social media and ecommerce is all in one neat package making it easy for your customers and prospects to do business with you. Social media is tied right to your app so that your customers can further communicate and attach themselves to your company. Right from your mobile app, we can drive them to your social media and they can like or add you as a friend further extending your brand.

Social media is also powerful because it is the number one way people share things in their life. They share restaurants, businesses, products, services, charities, clothes, bars, restaurants and on and on. We share things we like or believe in so it makes sense to attach your businesses social media to your mobile app so people will share and take action through your app. Social media has great power and so it makes sense to tie it into your mobile app as you not only need to get a mobile app but you have to market a mobile app as that is how you will get more downloads and new prospects. You do not want to be at the bottom of the pile. You want to rise to the top so people will discover your business when they do a search.

The self-design and publish platform of GenEpoch makes it easy to add your social media as there are powerful plug ins for your social media like Facebook, twitter and YouTube. You simply click a button and add it in to your offering. They make it as easy as possible to add in your social media with no programming experience. I hope you are beginning to see why we love this platform so much. It literally saves us on an average over 40 hours of programming because there are no programming skills needed.

17.2. Apple Versus Google

People often ask us what is the difference between Apple and Google and why are some on one and not the other? First of all one of the biggest difference between the two stores and companies is that Apple has much tighter controls on what they will allow on the Apple store. The second biggest difference between the two is that Google has way more mobile apps published than Apple. Do you see the connection? It is not for us to judge but some only care about Google because of more apps and oh yes more android based phones sold. Our strategy is that you do not want to miss out on any prospects or business so you really want to be on both but Apple will be harder to get on even with our experience.

Google does not allow garbage in their store, but as of right they now do not have a ton of requirements to publish with them. They are also quicker about getting you up and running. Once your app is designed and ready to go, it generally takes about 48-72 hours to have you up and live. This is pretty quick compared to Apple where you can wait until up to 3 weeks give or take. We have not figured out why especially in light of the fact that Google has way more apps being published than Apple. If you are rejected by Apple, there is no preferential treatment as once you think you have fixed the issues, you will have to get back in line again and that can take up to 3 weeks as well.

No one knows which company has a better philosophy yet, but it seems to be working for both companies. In our opinion we think long term that Apple will relax some of their standards and Google will bring theirs up. As with most things this will even out everything considered and create a long term strategy.

Do not make this a battle over Apple or Google. This really is about getting on both stores and giving your business the best chance of being found.

17.3. Assistive Services – Affordable Option

If you want to save money, but you know that you will need help with some important parts like the graphics or in finishing up your app then we have a service that is called assistive services. The idea behind this is very simple; you get to design your own app on the platform while having an expert work with you to get it done right.

We have been building mobile appsfor a while and understand that not everyone is a graphic artist or understands what it will take it get your app on Apple. This is a great option to keep the cost down and get a dynamic looking app. You must be willing to do your part with this option as you will be responsible for the majority of the work.

This is a great option to have the assistance of a professional mobile app developer to work with in developing your mobile app. It is not a complete hand holding experience but delivers a lot of crucial help in this new creation and venture. You will be placed with a professional developer or designer depending on what you need.

17.4. Custom App Development – More Costly Option

If you are not interested in building your own mobile app and are more concerned about the dynamics and look of your app then you may want to have your app built for you. A custom app option will give you peace of mind that you will have an expert do what they do best. A mobile app designer will make sure that all of the pieces are taken into count and will gather what your desires are for your app.

The designer then goes to work and starts to build your companies new mobile application and uses all available resources to implement and deploy a mobile app that will extend your brand and help return on your investment.

The savings are passed onto you because of the use of the advancement of technology. This helps to take away a lot of leg work and programming. This equates to about a 300% to 500% savings for your bottom line. We put our app building experience to work designing and building your app in the fashion that we know will have the best chance to get approved by Apple and Google. You go with the custom option because your time is valuable and you do not feel comfortable building your own app.

17.5. Creating a Functional Mobile App

What is a functional app? You might be looking through the App store and are looking for what a functional app is. As you look through all of the choices you are not really sure what that could mean as they all seem to function and we wouldn't disagree with you. Apple has set this standard and what they are looking for in order for you to be able to have your app publish on their store.

The idea is great and helps not only the business owner but other app developers and Apple as well. Here is what Apple is looking for and why they have this idea in mind.

Apple is looking for you to produce an Application that has purpose and meaning. Your app should serve some kind of entertainment, or information that is valuable or function like ordering a book or buying some electronics.

The reason for having a function is that they are looking for apps where people will come back to your app over and over again. They have done their research and know that apps that serve a function will produce this kind of result. They do not allow apps for instance for a wedding party. They know at some point the function is going to end like once the wedding has happened.

If you try and create a mobile app that is really all just about information that is considered just straight marketing in nature, then Apple will more than likely reject your app. It is obvious that you have a business and that you want people to discover your business but Apple says that is not enough and you can use a website for that purpose. A mobile app should be able to have some interaction taking place like: a tip calculator and a menu to order from. A mortgage calculator and a list of homes for sale for potential buyers are helpful. Provide a daily tip or quote and a way for customers to buy a book or program from you. This is a true function and you need to consider it when having your mobile app designed.

18. Tips on Helping You Get Your Mobile App Published on the Apple

Building and designing a mobile app can be tough enough but then you have to get it published in the Apple App Store. Getting it published can be a frustrating and long process. With our experience we would like to give you some tips on making this process easier and hopefully making the review process go smoother.

First step to this process is submitting your app and waiting for it to get uploaded to your Apple Developer account which can take up to 72 hours. You will then be notified by Apple that your app is waiting to be reviewed. The review time process on an average can take up to 7 to 15 days. The next email you receive from Apple will let you know whether or not they approved your app or rejected it. When they reject it they will post generic messages of why your app was not approved. They never really go into too much detail and sometimes leave you guessing as to why your app was not approved. This is why we would like to share with you some tips that will help you get your app approved or at least make the process a lot less frustrating.

*Disclaimer: These tips we are sharing are only to help you in the process of getting your app approved, but are not a guarantee as Apple is always changing their review process. These tips are just what we have experienced when submitting apps to the App Store.

Tip #1: When building your app be sure to make the first 5 tabs iPhone native.

Tip #2: Keep your mobile app simple (bare essentials) for the review process and then you can make changes after your app has been approved.

Tip #3: The Apple App Store will not accept any marketing mobile apps or any promoting mobile apps.
If you want your app to be approved you will have to build an app that is not displaying the marketing
side of your business but maybe instead you can show products and have it based around that idea.

Tip #4: Use high resolution images throughout your mobile app.

Tip #5: Use two to three colors to design your app and be sure to have your buttons and headers match your color scheme as well so that the design flows throughout the entire app.

Tip #6: If you are a non-profit organization, do not add any donation button within the app. Instead of a donate tab you can add a volunteer tab. After your app has been approved you can make changes.

Tip #7: Make sure your app has a nice presentation and quality content throughout.

Tip #8: Make sure that there are no broken links anywhere in your app.

Tip #9: Be sure to add content on all active tabs; do not leave any tabs blank.

Tip #10: Help your app stand out from the competition by writing a good description of what your app is about. The description is a very important tool in helping you promote your app as well as getting it approved on the App Store.
Tip #11: Be sure to add images to all of the ios features.

See Apple's Review Guidelines

18.1. App Reviews

The key to getting your mobile app more exposure in the App Store is getting as many customer reviews as you can. You have a better chance of being featured in the App Store listings when you have lots of positive reviews for your app. There are many ways to get great reviews. Here are some simple ways to get started:

1. Share your app with friends and family (ask them to give reviews in App Store and Google Play)
2. Share your app on all your social networks such as Facebook, twitter, Google+ and Pinterest.

3. Create a mobile app trailer and post to video sites such as YouTube and Vimeo. Be sure to share your video with all of your networks.

4. Submit your app to free app review sites (see below for the review sites we think will give you the best exposure).

18.2. Best App Review Sites

Freshapps: Favorite for app developers as it gives your app a lot of exposure. Reviewers can rate, vote, and comment on your app.

148apps: In-depth reviews to help readers evaluate an app's performance. This site will also notify you of an app price drop.

The iPhone App Review: Honest reviews of the most interesting iPhone apps out there. This site cannot review every app as there are too many but they will showcase the most original and exciting apps the App Store has to offer.

The Daily App Show: provides video iPhone, iPad, Mac and Android App Reviews to help you find new apps and read reviews before making an app purchase.

Iusethis: This site uses a more democratic way to rate apps. Instead of star ratings they go by the number of users to define the value of an app. Great web site to submit your app.

What's On IPHONE: This Network covers everything new in smartphones and tablets, with a special focus on iPhone, iPad, Android and mobile apps. You can choose these different options: expedited review, highlighted review, featured review, and spotlight review.

18.3. What is (PNS) or Push Notification System?

Do you remember the fad called text message marketing? Seemed like a great idea as the cell phone became more popular and a part of our everyday life. So some smart people gathered together and decided to charge businesses money to send out text messages in order to market their business. The idea seemed sound and a new industry was born. It has had its strengths but was seriously flawed from the beginning.

There are text messages we love to get and those we are not so found of. We love getting texts from our friends and family and we use it to communicate short messages to other associates and employees but having commercial messages come into our text message inbox seems to annoy most people and the call to action is just not there. If you send a great discount maybe I will act but overall the appearance of a text message is bland and a nuisance so back to the drawing board.

Luckily for you and me the drawing board was good to us as a better way to send out those important messages was created and without annoying people in the process. The birth of PNS or push notification system is like text message marketing on steroids, but is well thought out and designed with all of the great features in mind.

When you have your mobile app designed and launched, you will have the ability to deploy the PNS as a part of your mobile app. The way that PNS works is you sit down at your computer and you designed a message. This message is an offering or call to action or an announcement of a new product or service. Once you are done, you hit send and away it goes to everyone who has downloaded your mobile app. The message appears in the status bar and when the receiver wants to open they click on it and your mobile app doesn't even have to be open to do so. This makes your message important for you or your business, but not a nuisance to your customers.

With the PNS you can even postdate your messages to go out when you want them to. This is what makes this powerful as you have the ability to customize your messages as well as pre-set messages to go out regardless of how busy you are at the time. This makes your time even more valuable as you have an always on salesperson who will deliver your valuable messages.

18.4. Mobile Commerce & Engagement Statistics

47% of consumers confirm they use their smartphone to search for local information, such as information about a local store they want to visit. 46% of consumers look up prices on a store's mobile site, and 42% check inventory prior to shopping in the store (Source: Local and the e-tailing group, 2012)

Nearly two of three shoppers use at least one device to research and purchase while shopping, and 28% use two devices at a time. More than one in three shoppers made at least one purchase with their mobile devices during the past six months, and tablet shoppers have an even higher propensity to make a purchase on the device, with one in four having purchased six times or more in the past six months (Source: Local and the e-tailing group, 2012)

The number of US mobile phone owners who have used 2D barcodes in the past 3 months increased from 1% in 2010 to 5% in 2011 and reached 15% among smartphone users (Source: Forrester, 2011)

62% of shoppers search for deals digitally for at least half of their shopping trips (Source:GMA/Booz & Company Shopper Survey)

50% of U.S. cellphone users have smartphones (Source: Nielsen, 2012)

55 percent of consumers express an interest in mobile coupons but only 10 percent have actually received one from a merchant (Source:Mercator Advisory Group, 2012)

66% of Americans ages 24-35 own a smartphone (Source: Nielsen, 2012)

18 percent of consumers have redeemed a mobile coupon in the past 90 days (Source: Mobile Audience Insights Report from   jiWire, Feb 2012)

21 percent of consumers search for a coupon on their mobile device while in a store (Source:Mobile Audience Insights Report from JiWire, 2012)

80 percent of mobile users prefer locally relevant advertising and 75 percent are more likely to take an action after seeing a location-specific message (Source: Mobile Audience Insights Report from JiWire, 2012)

52% of adult cell phone owners use their devices while in a store to get help with purchasing decisions (Source: Pew American & Internet Life Project, 2012)

1.2 billion apps were downloaded during the holiday week between December 25-31 (Source: Flurry, 2011)
On Cyber Monday, 10.8% of people used a mobile device to visit a retailer's site, up from 3.9% in 2010. Additionally, mobile sales grew dramatically, reaching 6.6% on Cyber Monday versus 2.3% in 2010 (Source: IBM's fourth annual Cyber Monday Benchmark, 2011)

Sixty-five percent of mobile users said they used their mobile device to find a business to make an in-store purchase (Source: Google, 2011)

Forty-three percent of mobile shoppers have downloaded a retail app (Source: Retrevo, 2011)

Approximately 52 percent of smartphone users will use their device to research products, redeem coupons and use apps to assist in their holiday gift purchase (Source: Acquity Group, 2011)

Sixty-seven percent of consumers plan to make a purchase via mobile this holiday season (Source: PayPal, 2011)

As of 7pm ET on Black Friday, the number of consumers using a mobile device to visit a retailer's site was holding firm at 17.04% (Source: IBM Smarter Commerce, 2011)

As of 7pm ET on Black Friday,the number of consumers using their mobile device to make a purchase was holding steady at 9.51% (Source: IBM Smarter Commerce, 2011)

For Black Friday sales, iPhone continued to lead all mobile device traffic at 6.58 %, followed by Android at 5.20% and iPad at 4.71% (Source: IBM Smarter Commerce, 2011)

In terms of the types of information mobile users will be looking for via their devices this holiday season, 31 percent said they will look for updates on sales and promotions, 27 percent will look for local store hours and directions, 26 percent will seek out product information and availability, 26 percent will be interested in product photos, 18 percent will search for official retailer apps and 17 percent will use mobile for customer support. (InMobi Holiday Mobile Shopping Study)

29 percent of users will look to mobile devices to learn about new products or services, 27 percent will use their handset when making a purchasing decision and 15 percent of shoppers will use their mobile device to make a purchase while in a store this holiday season. (InMobi Holiday Mobile Shopping Study)

Not only will consumers use mobile to research products but, over 21 million, or 36 percent, plan to make purchases directly from their mobile devices. (InMobi Holiday Mobile Shopping Study)

Approximately 45 percent of mobile users plan to compare prices via their handsets during their Thanksgiving weekend shopping, up from 22 percent in 2010 (InMobi Holiday Mobile Shopping Study)

The percentage of shoppers buying from their mobile phones is expected to rise to 15% in November, compared to 4.5% in last year's holiday season, and less than 1% in 2009. In October, 9.6% of online shoppers made purchases through their mobile devices, up from 3.4% a year earlier. (IBM Coremetrics Forecast, 2011)

67% of consumers will use their smartphones to find store locations, 59% to compare prices, 51% to obtain product information, 46% to check product availability, 45% to read reviews, 45% to shop online, 41% to find and use coupons, 40% to scan bar codes, and 35% to access social media (Source: Deloitte's 2011 Annual Holiday Survey)

27% of smartphone owners will use their devices for holiday shopping this year

(Source: Deloitte's 2011 Annual Holiday Survey)

More than 60 percent of mobile buyers will make mobile purchases while at home (Source: Ipsos and PayPal Survey, 2011)

At least 46 percent of consumers plan to make mobile purchases this holiday season (Source: Ipsos and PayPal Survey, 2011)

53% of the "on-the-go" U.S. audience is willing to exchange their location in exchange for more relevant content and better information, including mobile deals (Source: JiWire, 2011)

More than 33.3 million U.S. consumers already engage in shopping-related activities on their mobile phones, 7%, or 2.3 million, of those consumers have made a purchase on their devices, the report finds (Source: research firm Experian Simmons, 2011 Mobile Consumer Report)

24% of U.S. adult online iPhone users and 21% of Android users have used a shopping application in the past three months (Source: Forrester, 2011)
Nearly half of consumers (47%) have accessed customer reviews in store using their mobile device with men (55%) more likely to access these reviews in store than women (39%) (Source: Shop.org, comScore and Social Shopping Labs, 2011)

41% of smartphone owners have made a purchase from their mobile phone. Of those, 16% bought apparel; 15% food and beverages; 11% toys and games; 11% electronics; 8% home goods; 4% sporting goods; 4% books; 3% jewelry; and 8% other products (Source: Chadwick Martin Bailey, 2011)

46 percent of consumers have used their phone to get product information while in a store (Source: Briabe Media, 2011)

56 percent of people believe mobile can make the shopping experience more enjoyable (Source: Lightspeed Research, 2011)

58% of mobile shoppers are age 18-34 and 34% of mobile shoppers make $100,000 or more a year (Source: comScore/Millennial Media Mobile Retail Study, 2011)

13.1 million consumers access retail content via mobile phones with 8.2 million of those visiting mobile commerce websites (Source: comScore/Millennial Media Mobile Retail Study, 2011)

67 percent of retailers see value of having customers use their smartphones within the store and 41 percent said they perceive a lot of value in mobile in-store (Source: RSR Research, 2011)

31 percent of consumers research a product on their mobile device before buying it in-store, while 40 percent of consumers research a product from their smartphone before purchasing it online (Source: JiWire Mobile Audience Insights Report Q1 2011)

Retailers plan to spend $220.9 million this year on mobile (Source:Shop.org and Forrester Research report, 2011)

It is predicted that U.S. mobile shopping sales volume will reach $9 billion in 2011 (Source: InMobi study, 2011)

74 million consumers in the United States already shop from their mobile devices (Source: InMobi study, 2011)

78 percent of retailers plan to invest in mobile this year (Source: The E-tailing Group Inc, 2011)

59% of consumers use their phone to perform mobile shopping activities from home while 28% use their phone in the retail store to perform mobile shopping activities (Source: 2011 Experian Study)

47% of consumers who have made a mobile transaction in the past year expect the experience on their mobile devices to be better than the experience in-store, 80% expect the experience to be better than or equal to in-store and 85% expect the experience to be better than or equal to online using a laptop or desktop computer (Source: Harris Interactive & Tealeaf Survey, 2011)

Within the 49% of mobile users who have made a mobile purchase in the last six months, 84% look for local retailer information, 82% find online retailers, 73% find a specific manufacturer or product website, 71% learn about a product or service after seeing an ad, 68% find the best price for a product or service, and 63% search before purchasing in a store or from a catalog (Source: Performics 2011 Mobile Search Insights Study, conducted by ROI Research)

75% of heavy mobile users said mobile search makes their lives easier, 63% said access to mobile search has changed the way they gather information, and 32% said they use mobile search more than search engines on their computers (Source: Performics 2011 Mobile Search Insights Study, conducted by ROI Research)

Over 70% of iPhone owners report using applications or their smartphone's web browser to help them while shopping in-store, and 41% are making purchases directly from their phones (Source: Chadwick Martin Bailey and iModerate Research Technologies, 2011)

48% of consumers conceded they use their mobile devices to look up product ratings or to find promotions (Source: Oracle, 2011)

49% of consumers who use the mobile web at least once a week made a purchase on their mobile device in the past six months (Source: ROI Research Inc., 2011)

In 3 years, it is predicted that 24% of retailers will have annual sales of 15% or greater coming from their mobile channel (Source: RSR Research, 2011)

51% of consumers say they have made a mobile payment within the past 3 months and 82% see themselves making one within the next year (Source: Mobio Identity Systems Inc. Report, 2011)

78-84% of consumers now rely on their social networks when researching new products (Source: IBM Report, 2011)

62% of smartphone users said they have purchased physical goods from their mobile devices in the last six months (Source: Adobe Survey, 2011)

Among smartphone owners, 48 percent prefer to visit a retailer's mobile website
and 38 percent prefer a mobile application
(Source: InsightExpress, 2010)

By 2015, it is predicted that mobile shopping will account for $163 billion in sales worldwide, 12% of global ecommerce turnover (Source: ABI Research, 2010)

Mobile alerts drive 1 out of 3 recipients in-store and 27% of those make a purchase (Source: Harris Interactive survey commissioned by Placecast, 2010)

The mobile retail market is predicted to exceed $12 billion by 2014 (Source: Juniper Research, 2010)

73% of companies are planning an investment in mobile channels in 2011, with almost half planning to move into mobile commerce (Source: Econsultancy's Customer Engagement Report)

69% of retail executives said mobile is an important strategic initiative (Source: NRF 2010)

Mobile commerce showed 86% year-over-year growth from 2010 to 2011 (Source: Appcelerator and IDC as reported by Mobile Commerce Daily)

Mobile barcode scanning increased 1,600% in 2010 (Source: Scanbuy as reported by Mobile Commerce Daily)

Consumers are 51% more likely to purchase from retailers that have mobile-specific websites (via Mobile Shopper session at NRF 2011)

79% of smartphone users found it useful to download mobile coupons to their phones (Source: Accenture, reported by Internet Retailer, 2010)

73% of consumers find it useful to receive an instant coupon as they pass by an item in a store (Source: Accenture, reported by Internet Retailer, 2010)

56% of shoppers with smartphones believe using their phone during the shopping experience will make it more enjoyable (Source: Accenture, reported by Internet Retailer, 2010)

US mobile commerce sales predicted to reach $3.4 billion this year (Source: ABI Research, 2010)

18.5. Mobile Industry Stats

By 2015, 81% of U.S. cell users will have smartphones (Source: Goldman Sachs, 2011)

Android expected to have 31pc market share by 2016 (Source: IDC, 2012)

53% of American consumers use their smartphones to access search engines at least once a day (Source: Google and Mobile Marketing Association Survey)

Globally, 80% of consumers have used computers to access the Web within the previous seven days. Sixty percent used their mobile devices to do so (Source: Google and the Mobile Marketing Association Survey)

By the end of 2011, Android is predicted to have nearly 40% of the total global market share, with Symbian at just over 20%, the iOS platform with 16% and RIM 14.9% (Source: IDC 2011 report)

US mobile subscriptions officially crossed the 100% penetration mark in Q4 2010 (Source: Chetan Sharma Consulting)

The smartphone market is now larger than the PC market. Smartphones outsold PCs in Q4 of 2010 101 million to 92 million (Source: IDC)

Smartphones and tablet computers will increase mobile Web traffic by 26 times during the next four years (Source: Cisco Systems, 2011) 86% of mobile internet users use their mobile device while watching TV with 37% of those browsing the internet for non-related TV material (Source: Yahoo, 2011)

The number of Smartphone users worldwide is predicted to exceed 1 billion by 2014 (Parks Associates, 2010)

25% of US mobile web users only access the web from their mobile phones
(Source: On Device Research, 2010 as reported by MobiThinking)

Mobile is predicted to be bigger than internet in 5 years (Morgan Stanley, 2010)

As you can see from all of the statistics, the mobile app industry is on a swift climb and the ROI from it is going to be incredible for your company. These are more than just numbers and talk as they tell a tale of something enormous happening!

Robert D. Kintigh

19. There is a Big Demand for App Brokers & Developers

Once you decide that you need a mobile app for your business, you may then be interested to know that there is a huge demand for mobile app brokers and developers. Maybe you could use some extra money or you may be looking to start a new business. If any of this is even remotely true then let me give you an idea about how big the opportunity is in the mobile app industry.

First of all, to go to work for someone as a mobile app sales person will bring you home upper five to six figures. As a mobile app developer you will probably start out at around 150k a year. If this is what the hired help is getting, imagine being the boss. This industry is exploding and it is barely getting started! The opportunity with mobile apps is growing daily and there is a demand for people who want to learn the business.

If this interest you then contact me through our website at www.truthmastery.com and we will point you in the right direction. If you are worried that you do not have the skills to do this, let me say that you will more than likely be ok if you want to learn on our platform. We will spend the time to teach you whatever aspect that you are looking to do.

We have a ton of people in our organization that will help you learn how to be a mobile app broker or how to develop the mobile apps. Once you get one for yourself and see how powerful they are, you may be excited to start something new or take on a new career. You never know but I also bet that you know someone who would be a perfect fit for the opportunity. If that is the case, please have them get in touch with me as well and have them let us know who referred them and we will take care of you for doing so.

So much has happened in the last couple of years and the ever expanding capabilities of the mobile app is exploding with possibilities. Our goal is to help as many small businesses as possible. These people who are just like you do not have enough time or resources and very rarely does a product or service come along that can actually help with both. Our services and products will actually not cost them an arm and a leg and will remove burden from them and not dump more on them. These people need help and you can be a part of it one way or another!

19.1. What Will the Future Hold?

No one really knows where the future will take us with mobile apps. The possibilities are endless with mobile apps because they are only limited by imagination. Over the next 3 years the experts and analyst state that the mobile app industry will grow to a 35 billion dollar industry and this might even be conservative as this is an industry that is exploding like no other.

It was not that long ago that all you could really do was place a call to someone on a cell phone. Then along came text messaging and eventually an idea called applications for your then smart phone. When the idea first came out, these applications when weight down your phone. You were limited on what you could download because of the capabilities of the mobile device. Today, you can literally download 100's of mobile applications to your smart device because of the way technology has advanced. These apps have increased the capabilities of your smart device as well as the device itself increasing. The two together make an extremely powerful combination.

So what have you decided? Do you want to get a mobile app for your business? Do you see all of the power that it possesses and what it could do for your bottom line? Have you provided you with enough information to make an intelligent buying decision? Have you begun to dream about what yours will look like? How will you market your new app?

Maybe we have shown you enough even that you have some interest in becoming a mobile app broker or developer. There are quite a few businesses that are a great fit to also sell mobile apps as a second or additional means of income. Businesses like SEO companies, web development companies, social media companies, business coaches, and more. Maybe you are not in a related industry but just want to create an additional stream of income. That is perfectly fine as we can help you do just that. This platform is for most people and these services are badly needed.

The time has come one way or another to get in the game and take part in the revolution. Businesses will be made during this time period of great expansion. It really doesn't matter what side of the equation you are on as long as you are in the game. Do not make the mistake of avoiding something because it is new and you are afraid of it. We wrote this book to make you better informed. Now that you are armed with the best information, take a step forward and get started. We have a huge team behind us to help you achieve your goals.

19.2. Marketing Your Mobile App

Once you have built your mobile app on the platform and you are loading it up for review, you are able to add keywords in order to help get your app found. This is the beginning of where the marketing starts with your mobile app. We need several aspects to happen in order for you to get found on both stores and drive more prospects to your business. The keywords are just a start. These keywords work very similar to keywords used to get found online. You attach the keywords that help you to get found.

Next comes sending out emails to your current customers and have them to download your mobile app and leave a review. Reviews are very important as the more relevant that you appear, then the higher you show up in search results. Ask them to write a review for you. If you do not ask you may not get so do not be afraid to ask for a review from a loyal customer. If you have served them well, they will be more than happy to help out. Reviews are tough to get even from family members so don't be too tough on those who say they will help. It is still kind of a mystery why more people do not follow through on giving reviews but they don't perform so well. All I can say is stay persistent on this.

Next is social media that you can use to get your mobile app downloaded and reviewed. You need to consistently promote your mobile app and ask people to download your app and leave a review. Watch out being too "*salesy*" when you promote your app. The tactic

I use the most is to ask for help from my connections. Make sure you reciprocate when they need help. This is a powerful motive for people as they love to help out but they will not put up with "takers" so make sure it is give and take.

Find groups that support app reviews and do your part. These are great sites as long as again it is give and take. Be honest in your reviews back. Bad reviews are a black mark towards you so make sure that you know what you are talking about. Also, leave real feedback so look through the whole app.

Make sure your own app is on your phone or tablet and carry it around with you. Every chance you get, ask people to take a look at your mobile app and then see if they will leave a review for you. The easier you make it the better. We like to put the review tabs right on the app. By having your app on you at all times, you can also get people to take a look at what you have to offer. Show them your products or services.

Ask people at your church if they will download your app and leave a review. Show them that you are running an honest and quality business. They will love to support your efforts if they feel your sincerity.

Put your mobile app on your website with the ability to download to itunes or the Google Play store. Put it on your blog or any piece of marketing where people will see your offering. Talk about your mobile app so they can understand why they want to download it. Again, ask for a review once they do and look through it.

Create a video about your app and put it on YouTube or Vimeo. Take screen shots and narrate what people are looking at and then send the video around.

19.3. About the Authors

Robert & Sallie Kintigh have over ten years' experience in the internet marketing field and since 2008 have had great experience in the mobile app arena. Robert has previously published two books called The Lies We Tell Ourselves and On the Run How to

Investigate and Find Your Runaway Teen. Robert has a love for writing and is driven to bring books to the market place that delivers value to his readers.

Robert has a background in technical writing as well as educational writing for businesses programs and seminars as well as corporate training programs. Robert has been a leader in the internet marketing field as well as the mobile app industry.

Sallie has a tremendous background in graphic design and her talents are on displays with all of Robert's books as well as the mobile apps that her company produces called SCM Web Team. Sallie has an eye for graphics and illustrations and makes sure that everything is right before they are deployed.

These two have come together to write a great book for all business owners and entrepreneurs who want to know more about the mobile app industry. Their talents come together in a dynamic way that has produced both a technical piece and a well thought out guide to the mobile app industry.

Look for more books to come from these two authors as they have a thirst for delivering the best written works and are very driven in their pursuit of helping people and businesses improve their daily lives. You can find out more at our website at www.truthmastery.com or about the mobile app platform at www.joingenepoch.com

www.ingramcontent.com/pod-product-compliance
Lightning Source LLC
Chambersburg PA
CBHW032009170526
45157CB00002B/622